DAY HIKES AROUND
SANTA BARBARA
CALIFORNIA

46 OF THE BEST

by Robert Stone

D0111391

Day Hike Books, Inc.
RED LODGE, MONTANA

Published by Day Hike Books, Incorporated
114 South Hauser Avenue
P.O. Box 865
Red Lodge, Montana 59068

Distributed by The Globe Pequot Press
6 Business Park Road
P.O. Box 833
Old Saybrook, CT 06475
www.globe-pequot.com
1-800-243-0495

Photographs by Robert Stone
Design by Paula Doherty

Cover photo:
Mission Creek and Little Fern Canyon Falls, Hikes 13, 14 and 15.
Back cover photo: Seven Falls, Hike 15.

TABLE OF CONTENTS

— THE HIKES —

THE FRONT COUNTY

THE UPPER COUNTRY
Camino Cielo Road and the Santa Ynez Ridge

Upper Santa Ynez Area

Lower Santa Ynez Area
Paradise Road

Cachuma Lake Area

About the Hikes

Santa Barbara, known as the "jewel of the American Riviera," is a charming oceanfront city surrounded by a diverse landscape and a considerable number of hiking trails. To the north of the coast, the Santa Ynez Mountains rise 3,000 feet, serving as a backdrop to Santa Barbara and nearby coastal communities. These mountains separate the coastal plain from the rolling farmlands and mountainous interior of Santa Barbara County. This guide will take you to 46 of the best day hikes in this area, getting you to the trailhead and onto the trail with clear, concise directions.

The network of hiking trails around Santa Barbara stretch along the coast, up and over the Santa Ynez Mountains, and throughout the Santa Ynez River Valley. The hikes in this guide include waterfalls, hot springs, swimming holes, lakes, creeks, deep canyons, extraordinary sandstone formations, nature preserves, coastal bluffs, architectural ruins, and scenic overlooks with panoramic views. These beautiful areas can often be enjoyed for the whole day. To help you decide which hikes are most appealing to you, a brief summary of the highlights is included with each hike.

Most of these hikes are found within a short drive of Santa Barbara. A map of all the hikes can be found on pages 6—7. A map of the upper region is on pages 60—61. Each of the hikes is also accompanied with its own map and detailed driving and hiking directions. The U.S.G.S. maps and other supplementary maps listed with the hikes are not necessary but may be useful for some areas. Many of the U.S.G.S. maps have not been updated recently, and the trails may not be shown. However, these maps are interesting because they show the topography of the region.

Be sure to wear comfortable hiking shoes, and be prepared for inclement weather. Sunscreen, insect repellent, and drinking water are highly recommended.

Hiking around Santa Barbara will give you a new appreciation of the beauty of this region. Enjoy your day hike as you discover southern California out on the trails!

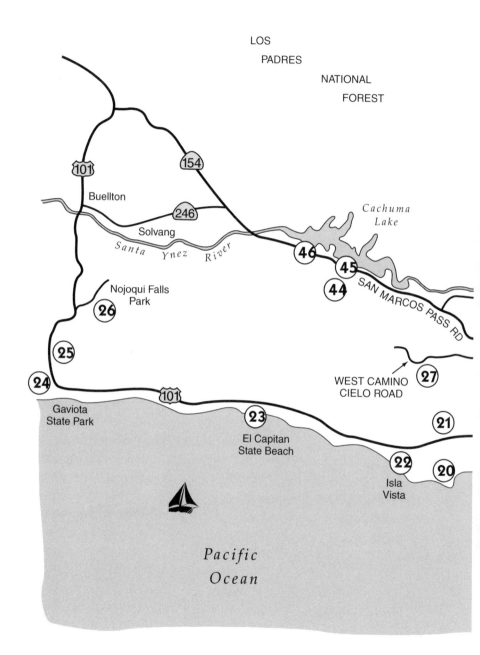

LOS
PADRES
NATIONAL
FOREST

101

154

Buellton

246

Solvang

Santa Ynez River

Cachuma
Lake

46

45

44

SAN MARCOS PASS RD

Nojoqui Falls
Park

26

25

24

WEST CAMINO
CIELO ROAD

27

101

Gaviota
State Park

23

El Capitan
State Beach

21

22

20

Isla
Vista

Pacific
Ocean

MAP
OF THE HIKES

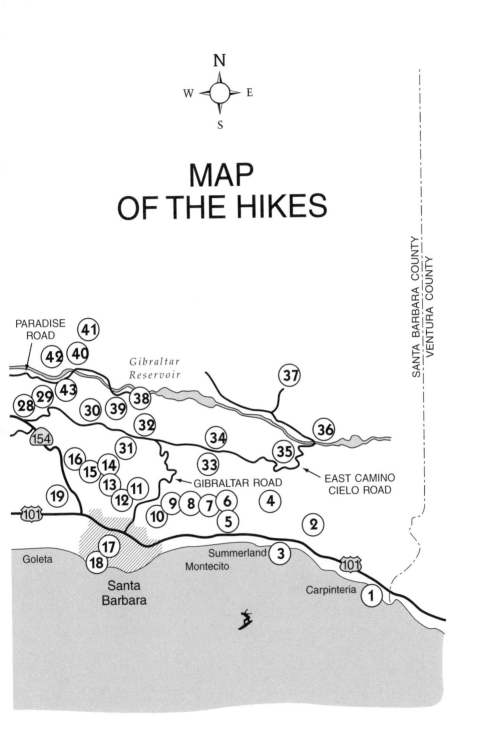

Hike 1
Carpinteria Bluffs
and Seal Sanctuary

Hiking distance: 2 miles round trip
Hiking time: 1 hour
Elevation gain: Level
Maps: The Thomas Guide—Santa Barbara & Vicinity
U.S.G.S. Carpinteria

Summary of hike: The Carpinteria Bluffs and Seal Sanctuary is an incredible spot. The bluffs offer great views overlooking the ocean, while the trail looks down at a community of harbor seals on the shore. You can watch the seals playing in the water, lounging, and sunbathing on the rocks and shoreline. The sanctuary is a protected birthing habitat for harbor seals during the winter and spring from December 1 through May 31.

Driving directions: From Highway 101 in Carpinteria, exit on Bailard Avenue. Drive one block south towards the ocean, and park at the road's end.

Hiking directions: From the end of the road, hike south on the well-worn path across the open meadow towards the ocean. As you near the ocean cliffs, take the pathway to the right, parallel to a row of stately eucalyptus trees. At the west end of the eucalyptus grove, bear left and cross the railroad tracks. The trail resumes across the tracks, heading to the right. (For an optional side trip, take the beach access trail on the left down to the base of the cliffs.) Continue west along the edge of the ocean bluffs to a bamboo fence—the seal sanctuary overlook. After enjoying the seals and views, return along the same path.

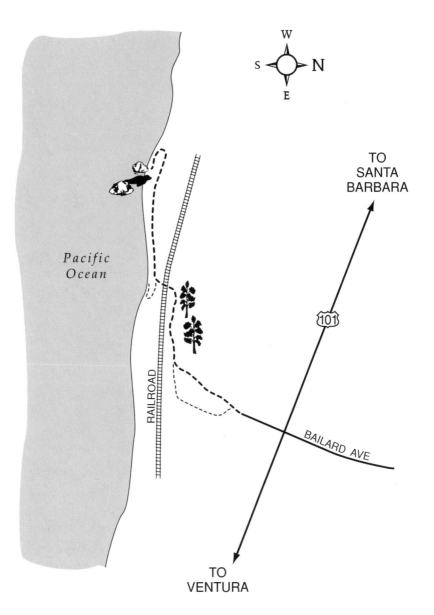

W
S —✦— N
E

TO
SANTA
BARBARA

Pacific
Ocean

RAILROAD

101

BAILARD AVE

TO
VENTURA

CARPINTERIA BLUFFS
AND
SEAL SANCTUARY

Hike 2
Toro Canyon Park

Hiking distance: 1 mile round trip
Hiking time: 30 minutes
Elevation gain: 300 feet
Maps: The Thomas Guide—Santa Barbara & Vicinity
U.S.G.S. Carpinteria

Summary of hike: Toro Canyon Park, located in the foothills between Carpinteria and Summerland, takes in 74 acres of oak woodland, native chaparral, and sandstone outcroppings. There are shady picnic spots under the trees and along the stream. The hike circles a knoll and heads up to a gazebo with panoramic 360-degree views of the coastline, mountains, and orchards.

Driving directions: From Santa Barbara, drive southbound on Highway 101 to Summerland and exit on North Padaro Lane. Drive north one block to Via Real and turn right. Continue 0.4 miles to Toro Canyon Road and turn left. Drive 1.3 miles to the signed Toro Canyon Park turnoff and turn right. Proceed one mile to Toro Canyon Park on the left. Turn left and drive 0.2 miles to the trail sign at the upper end of the park. Park by the sandstone outcropping on the right.

Hiking directions: From the parking area, hike north past the trail sign and across the stream towards the prominent sandstone formation. From the outcropping, take the wide, uphill path to the right. At 0.3 miles is a trail split, which is the beginning of the loop. Hiking clockwise, take the left fork around the small knoll and up to a gazebo at the hilltop. After enjoying the beautiful views, continue to the west, completing the loop around the hill. Return to the left, back to the trailhead.

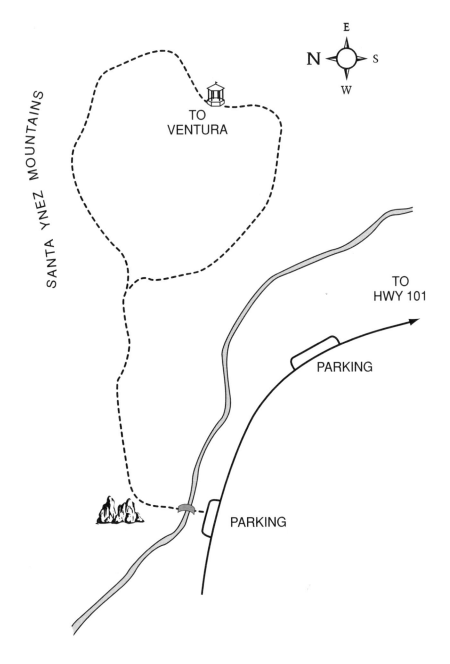

E
N — S
W

TO
VENTURA

SANTA YNEZ MOUNTAINS

TO
HWY 101

PARKING

PARKING

TORO CANYON PARK

Hike 3
Summerland Beach
from Lookout Park

Hiking distance: 1-mile loop
Hiking time: 30 minutes
Elevation gain: 50 feet
Maps: The Thomas Guide—Santa Barbara & Vicinity
U.S.G.S. Carpinteria

Summary of hike: Lookout Park is a beautiful, grassy flat along the oceanfront cliffs in Summerland. From the park, paved walkways and natural forested trails lead down to a sandy beach, creating a one-mile loop. A short distance up the coast from the beach are tidepools and coves.

Driving directions: From Santa Barbara, drive southbound on Highway 101 and take the Summerland exit. Turn right (south), crossing the railroad tracks in one block, and park in the Lookout Park parking lot.

Coming from the south, heading northbound on Highway 101, take the Evans Avenue exit and turn left. Cross Highway 101 and the railroad tracks to Lookout Park.

Hiking directions: From the parking lot, head left (east) through the grassy flat along the cliffs' edge to an open gate. A path leads through a shady eucalyptus tree forest. Cross a wooden bridge, and head to the sandy shoreline. At the shore, bear to the right, leading to the paved walkways that return up to Lookout Park. To extend the hike, continue along the coastline to the west. At low tide, the long stretch of beach leads to coves, rocky points, and tidepools.

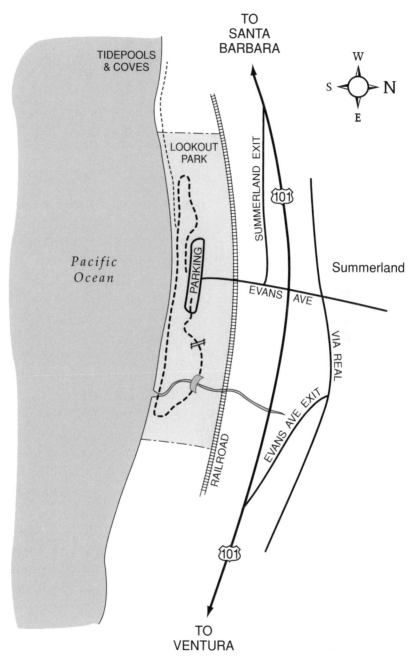

TO
SANTA
BARBARA

TIDEPOOLS
& COVES

W

S — N

E

LOOKOUT
PARK

SUMMERLAND EXIT

101

Summerland

Pacific
Ocean

PARKING

EVANS   AVE

VIA REAL

EVANS AVE EXIT

RAILROAD

101

TO
VENTURA

SUMMERLAND BEACH

Hike 4
Romero Canyon Trail

Hiking distance: 6-mile loop
Hiking time: 3 hours
Elevation gain: 1,400 feet
Maps: Santa Barbara Front Country Recreational Map
U.S.G.S. Carpinteria

Summary of hike: The Romero Canyon Trail follows Romero Creek up a narrow, secluded, shady canyon past pools and a waterfall. The hike returns on scenic Romero Canyon Road, an old fire road overlooking the canyon and the coastline.

Driving directions: From Santa Barbara, drive southbound on Highway 101, and exit on Sheffield Drive in Montecito. Turn right and drive 1.3 miles to East Valley Road. Turn left and quickly turn right on Romero Canyon Road. Continue 1.5 miles (bearing right at 0.4 miles) to Bella Vista Road and turn right. Drive a quarter mile to a horseshoe bend in the road. The trailhead is at this bend on the left by a steel gate.

Hiking directions: Hike past the gate on the fire road on the east side of Romero Creek. After a quarter mile, cross the wide bridge over the creek. At 0.4 miles is a second creek crossing and a junction. The left fork leads west to San Ysidro Canyon. Go to the right on the main trail to another creek crossing a hundred yards ahead. After crossing, leave the main trail and take the left fork, following the "trail" sign up Romero Canyon. The trail runs parallel to the creek, crossing boulders by pools and a waterfall at 1.3 miles. A short distance ahead, two streams converge, and the trail crosses the stream. At 1.7 miles, switchbacks lead up to the Romero Canyon Road. Take the road to the right, beginning a four-mile descent along the hillside overlooking the canyon. The loop is completed at the canyon junction and creek crossing. Retrace your steps back to the trailhead.

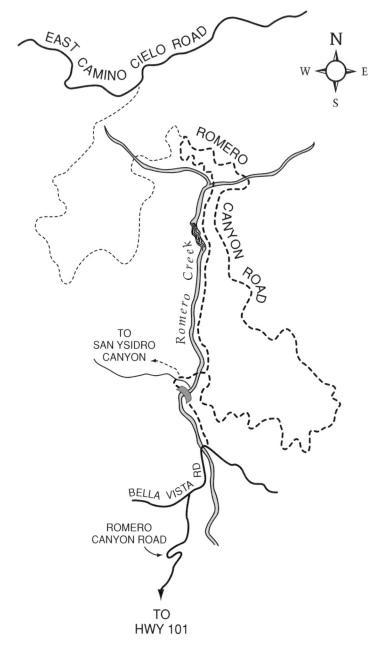

ROMERO CANYON TRAIL

Hike 5
San Ysidro Creekside Trail

Hiking distance: 2.4 miles round trip
Hiking time: 1.4 hours
Elevation gain: Near level
Maps: The Thomas Guide—Santa Barbara & Vicinity
U.S.G.S. Carpinteria

Summary of hike: The San Ysidro Creekside Trail, in the heart of Montecito, meanders through an oak, olive, and eucalyptus woodland. San Ysidro Creek flows through a 44-acre preserve under old stone bridges that span the creek.

Driving directions: From Santa Barbara, drive southbound on Highway 101 to Montecito, and exit on San Ysidro Road. Drive one block north to San Leandro Lane and turn right. Continue 0.7 miles to 1710 San Leandro Lane, and park alongside the road. En route to the trailhead, San Leandro Lane jogs to the left and back again to the right.

Hiking directions: From San Leandro Lane, hike north along the east bank of San Ysidro Creek for 100 yards to an old stone bridge crossing the creek. Instead of crossing, stay on the footpath to the right along the same side of the creek. At 0.4 miles, the trail joins Ennisbrook Drive for 100 yards before dropping back down to the forest and creek. Cross the stone bridge over San Ysidro Creek, continuing upstream to a junction. The left fork leads to a cul-de-sac at the south end of East Valley Lane. Bear to the right, crossing a stream through a lush, overgrown forest. At 1.2 miles is another signed junction. The left fork also leads to East Valley Lane. Take the right fork and cross San Ysidro Creek. Once across, the trail winds through a eucalyptus forest and ends a short distance ahead at private property. To return, reverse your route.

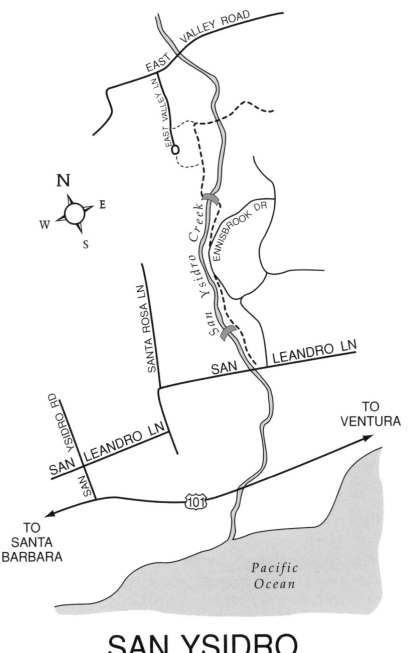

EAST VALLEY ROAD

EAST

EAST VALLEY LN

San Ysidro Creek

ENNISBROOK DR

N

E

W

S

SANTA ROSA LN

SAN LEANDRO LN

SAN YSIDRO RD

SAN LEANDRO LN

SAN

TO
VENTURA

101

TO
SANTA
BARBARA

*Pacific
Ocean*

SAN YSIDRO
CREEKSIDE TRAIL

Hike 6
San Ysidro Canyon

Hiking distance: 3.7 miles round trip
Hiking time: 2 hours
Elevation gain: 1,200 feet
Maps: Santa Barbara Front Country Recreational Map
　　　　U.S.G.S. Carpinteria and Santa Barbara

Summary of hike: The San Ysidro Trail heads up the picturesque San Ysidro Canyon along the cascading San Ysidro Creek. The steep, narrow, upper canyon is filled with small waterfalls, continuous cascades, and pools. This hike leads to San Ysidro Falls, a beautiful 60-foot waterfall.

Driving directions: From Santa Barbara, drive southbound on Highway 101 to Montecito, and exit on San Ysidro Road. Drive one mile north to Valley Road and turn right. Continue 0.8 miles to Park Lane and turn left. Drive 0.3 miles to East Mountain Drive and bear to the left. The trailhead is 0.2 miles ahead on the right. Park along East Mountain Drive.

Hiking directions: The signed trail heads to the right (north), parallel to a wooden fence. Proceed on the tree-covered lane, past a few homes, to a paved road. Follow the road 100 yards uphill to an unpaved road and a chain link gate. Past the gate, the trail drops into San Ysidro Canyon. At a half mile, there is a trail junction with the McMenemy Trail on the left (Hike 7). Continue up the canyon on the fire road past another gate and Gateway Rock, a large, eroded sandstone wall on the left. A hundred yards beyond Gateway Rock, power lines cross high above the trail near another junction. Take the footpath bearing to the right, leaving the fire road. The trail gains elevation up the canyon past continuous cascades and pools. Several side paths lead to the left down to San Ysidro Creek. At 1.5 miles, a switchback and metal railing mark the beginning of the steeper ascent up canyon. The trail crosses a stream at 1.8 miles. To the right, is a short side scramble up the narrow canyon to various pools, falls, and cascades. Back on the main trail, continue 100 yards to a trail fork. The right fork leads to the base of San Ysidro Falls. This is our turn-around spot.

To hike further, the left fork climbs out of the canyon to the Camino Cielo Ridge, gaining 1,800 feet in 2.5 miles.

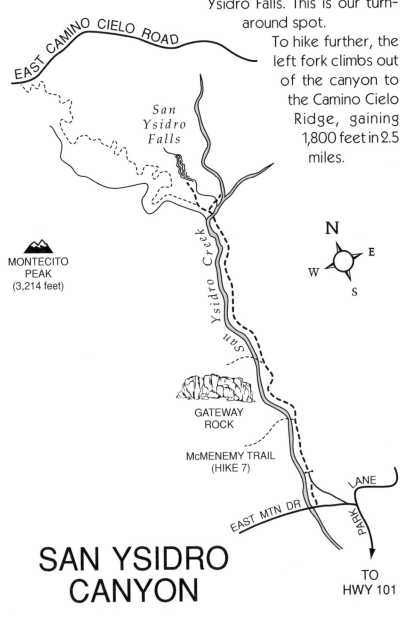

EAST CAMINO CIELO ROAD

San Ysidro Falls

N
E
W
S

MONTECITO PEAK
(3,214 feet)

Ysidro Creek

San

GATEWAY ROCK

McMENEMY TRAIL
(HIKE 7)

LANE

PARK

EAST MTN DR

SAN YSIDRO
CANYON

TO
HWY 101

Hike 7
McMenemy Trail

Hiking distance: 5.5 miles round trip
Hiking time: 3 hours
Elevation gain: 1,000 feet
Maps: Santa Barbara Front Country Recreational Map
U.S.G.S. Carpinteria and Santa Barbara

Summary of hike: The McMenemy Trail is a connector trail between San Ysidro Canyon and Hot Springs Canyon. This hike begins in the picturesque San Ysidro Canyon. The trail leads over the ridge between the canyons to meadows and scenic overlooks. It then descends into Hot Springs Canyon below Montecito Peak.

Driving directions: From Santa Barbara, drive southbound on Highway 101 to Montecito, and exit on San Ysidro Road. Drive one mile north to Valley Road and turn right. Continue 0.8 miles to Park Lane and turn left. Drive 0.3 miles to East Mountain Drive and bear to the left. The trailhead is 0.2 miles ahead on the right. Park along East Mountain Drive.

Hiking directions: The signed trail heads to the right (north), parallel to a wooden fence. Proceed on the tree-covered lane, past a few homes, to a paved road. Follow the road 100 yards uphill to an unpaved road and a chain link gate. Past the gate, the trail drops into San Ysidro Canyon. At a half mile, there is a trail junction with the signed McMenemy Trail on the left. Rock hop across San Ysidro Creek to the left. Head up a short hill to another junction. Take the left fork up to a meadow overlooking the ocean. Switchbacks lead up to a trail split. Both trails lead up McMenemy Hill to a ridge with a rock bench. There are first-class views up and down the coastline from this 1,250-foot perch. After a rest, proceed downhill past a water tank and rock outcroppings. Cross a small stream near a waterfall, and head to a signed junction. The right fork, Saddle Rock Trail, leads a short distance up to a garden of large sandstone boulders. The left fork leads 0.2 miles down to the unpaved Hot Springs Road and Hot Springs Creek. Both trails are worth exploring. To return, retrace your steps.

MONTECITO
PEAK
(3,214 feet)

SADDLE ROCK
TRAIL

HOT SPRINGS CANYON

Hot Springs Creek

ROCK
BENCH

WATER
TANK

Ysidro Creek

SAN YSIDRO CANYON

San

EAST MTN DR

W **N**
S **E**

PARK LANE

TO
HWY 101

McMENEMY TRAIL

Hike 8
Cold Spring Canyon
East Fork to Montecito Overlook

Hiking distance: 3.2 miles round trip
Hiking time: 1.5 hours
Elevation gain: 900 feet
Maps: Santa Barbara Front Country Recreational Map
U.S.G.S. Santa Barbara

Summary of hike: The hike up the East Fork of Cold Spring Canyon follows Cold Spring Creek through an alder, bay, and oak forest. Between the steep canyon walls are creek crossings, deep pools, and waterfalls. The destination is Montecito Overlook, a spectacular vista point that spans up and down the coast from the ocean to the mountains.

Driving directions: From Santa Barbara, drive southbound on Highway 101. Take the Hot Springs Road exit in Montecito and turn left. Drive 0.1 mile to Hot Springs Road and turn left again. Continue 2.2 miles to Mountain Drive and turn left. Drive 1.1 mile to the Cold Spring Trailhead on the right, located where the creek flows across the paved road. Park along the road.

Hiking directions: Access the trail from either side of Cold Spring Creek. Both trails join a short distance ahead on the east side of the creek. At a quarter mile is a bench, pool, and junction with the West Fork Trail on the left (Hike 9). Continue north on the same side of the creek. The trail gains elevation up the canyon to a creek crossing at 0.6 miles. Rock hop across the creek, and continue uphill through the shady forest past waterfalls and pools to another creek crossing at 0.8 miles. After crossing, switchbacks lead up the mountainside away from the creek. At 1.3 miles, the trail joins a utility service road. Take the road a short distance to the right and up onto a knoll— Montecito Overlook. This overlook is the destination.

To hike further, continue 100 yards along the service road to another junction with a trail veering off to the left. The trail leads two miles further to Montecito Peak (Hike 33), adding 1,550 feet to this hike.

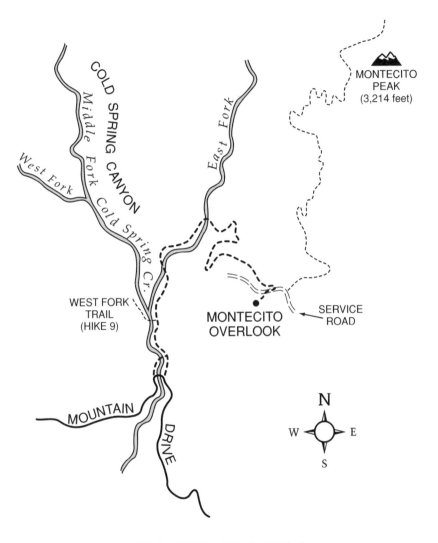

EAST FORK
COLD SPRING CANYON

Hike 9
Cold Spring Canyon
West Fork to Tangerine Falls

Hiking distance: 3.5 miles round trip
Hiking time: 2 hours
Elevation gain: 900 feet
Maps: Santa Barbara Front Country Recreational Map
U.S.G.S. Santa Barbara

Summary of hike: This hike up Cold Spring Canyon passes numerous cascades, pools, and waterfalls as the trail parallels the creeks. The forested hike includes an off-trail scramble up a gorge to a 200-foot waterfall known as Tangerine Falls.

Driving directions: From Santa Barbara, drive southbound on Highway 101. Take the Hot Springs Road exit in Montecito and turn left. Drive 0.1 mile to Hot Springs Road and turn left again. Continue 2.2 miles to Mountain Drive and turn left. Drive 1.1 mile to the Cold Spring Trailhead on the right, located where the creek flows across the paved road. Park along the road.

Hiking directions: Hike north along either side of Cold Spring Creek. Within minutes, both trails join on the east side of the creek. Proceed up canyon to a junction with the West Fork Cold Spring Trail on the left by a bench and small waterfall, located where two creeks merge. Cross the creek to the left, and head up the western wall of West Fork Canyon parallel to the creek. At 0.8 miles, an unsigned junction takes off to the right. Go to the right, leaving the main trail. Cross a seasonal creek and enter the Middle Fork Cold Spring Canyon. This side trail follows the creek past pools and waterfalls to the base of Tangerine Falls. This unmaintained trail is a scramble over boulders and old water pipes in a steep canyon. Use caution!

To hike further, return to the main trail. Continue for one mile to Gibraltar Road, climbing 700 feet out of the canyon.

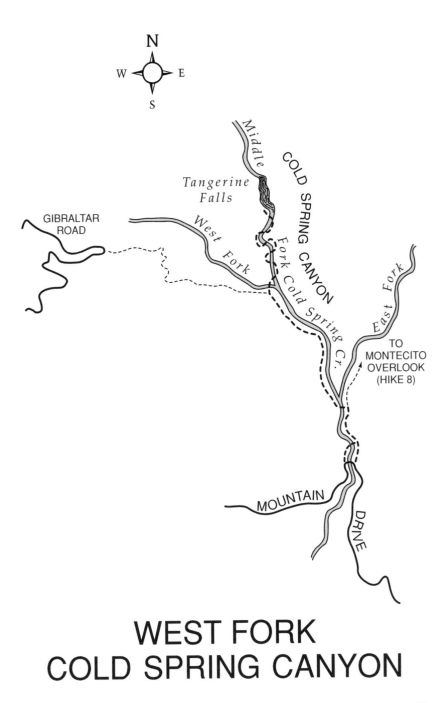

N
W E
S

Middle

COLD SPRING CANYON

Tangerine
Falls

GIBRALTAR
ROAD

West Fork

Fork Cold Spring Cr.

East Fork

TO
MONTECITO
OVERLOOK
(HIKE 8)

MOUNTAIN

DRIVE

WEST FORK
COLD SPRING CANYON

Hike 10
Parma Park

Hiking distance: 2.5-mile loop
Hiking time: 1.4 hours
Elevation gain: 300 feet
Maps: The Thomas Guide—Santa Barbara & Vicinity
　　　　 U.S.G.S. Santa Barbara

Summary of hike: Parma Park is a wonderful, undeveloped park in the foothills of Sycamore Canyon. Coyote Creek, Sycamore Creek, and several seasonal streams flow through the park. Some of the trails follow the lush, forested canyon with old growth trees; others lead to knolls overlooking the surrounding hills. The trails in the park are intentionally unmarked.

Driving directions: In Santa Barbara, take Sycamore Canyon Road north to Stanwood Drive and turn left. Drive 0.7 miles to Parma Park on the right. The parking lot gate is usually locked. Park across the road in the parking pullouts.

Hiking directions: Hike north past the entrance sign and gate, crossing an old stone bridge. At the end of the paved road, is an open area and a four-way junction. To the right, by the well, the unmarked Rowe Trail leads downhill and across the creek. Continue on this trail to the ridge above Stanwood Drive. Head east along the ridge, parallel to the road below. At the east end, the trail curves left to the Parma Fire Road on a knoll overlooking Sycamore Canyon, the Santa Ynez Mountains, and the ocean. Head left, returning along the fire road. The trail descends to a series of knolls and into a forested area in the canyon. Cross a seasonal stream, and complete the loop.

A second hiking trail heads north from the four-way junction. The trail crisscrosses a seasonal creek up a forested canyon. At 0.3 miles, the trail leaves the creek and switchbacks up to the ridge at Mountain Drive. Return along the same route.

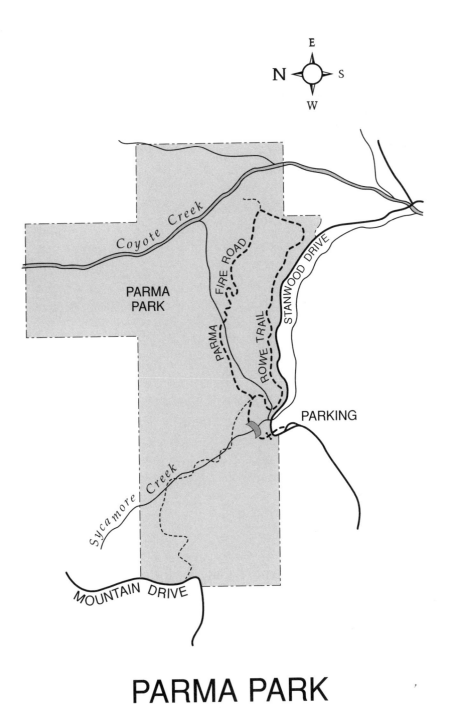

PARMA PARK

Hike 11
Rattlesnake Canyon

Hiking distance: 3.5 miles round trip
Hiking time: 2 hours
Elevation gain: 1,000 feet
Maps: Santa Barbara Front Country Recreational Map
    U.S.G.S. Santa Barbara

Summary of hike: Rattlesnake Canyon is one of Santa Barbara's most popular trails. The trail leads up the winding canyon through a lush, riparian forest with many pools, small waterfalls, and stream crossings. There is a grotto, meadow, and a panoramic vista overlooking the Pacific Ocean and the Channel Islands. Rattlesnake Canyon received its name for its winding canyon, not for snake occupancy.

Driving directions: From the Santa Barbara Mission, take Mission Canyon Road north towards the mountains for 0.6 miles to Foothill Road—turn right. Drive 0.2 miles to Mission Canyon Road and turn left. Continue 0.5 miles to Las Conoas Road and turn sharply to the right, following the Skofield Park sign. Take this winding road 1.2 miles to the trailhead, located by a beautiful stone bridge over Rattlesnake Creek. Park in the pullouts along the right side of the road or a short distance ahead in Skofield Park.

Hiking directions: Head north past the trail sign along the west side of the stone bridge. Rock hop across the creek to a wide trail. Head to the left another half mile to a trail split. Continue straight ahead on the narrower trail, staying in the canyon and creek. Descend to the cascading Rattlesnake Creek and recross to the west side of the creek. The trail climbs out of the canyon via switchbacks. At 1.3 miles is the first of two successive creek crossings. Between these crossings are cascades, small waterfalls, pools, flat sunbathing boulders, and a rock grotto. Back on the west side of the watercourse, the trail climbs to Tin Can Meadow, a grassy flat with views of the surrounding mountains. Just beyond the meadow is a junction with the Tunnel Connector Trail. This is the turnaround spot. Return along the same path.

To hike further, take the right fork uphill to the east for 0.7 miles to Gibraltar Road, or take the left fork uphill to the west 0.8 miles to the Tunnel Trail in Mission Canyon (Hike 14).

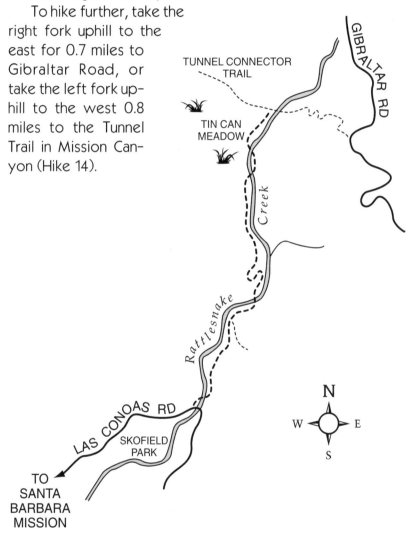

RATTLESNAKE CANYON

Hike 12
Santa Barbara Botanic Garden

Hiking distance: 2 miles round trip
Hiking time: 2 hours
Elevation gain: 50 feet
Maps: Santa Barbara Botanic Garden Visitors' Map
Guide to the Santa Barbara Botanic Garden

Summary of hike: The Santa Barbara Botanic Garden has seven looping nature trails totaling 5.5 miles. The trails cover a wide variety of habitats on the 65-acre grounds. Through the heart of the garden flows Mission Creek. The trails pass through a canyon, a redwood forest, over bridges, past a waterfall, and across a historic dam built in 1906. This hike is only a suggested route. Many other paths can be chosen to view areas of your own interests.

Driving directions: From the Santa Barbara Mission, take Mission Canyon Road north towards the mountains for 0.6 miles to Foothill Road—turn right. Drive 0.2 miles to Mission Canyon Road and turn left. Continue 0.9 miles to the Botanic Garden parking lot on the left at 1212 Mission Canyon Road.

Hiking directions: From the entrance, head to the right past a pond and through a meadow. Past the meadow is the Redwood Forest. (The Woodland Trail is a side loop to the east.) The trail leads downhill towards Mission Creek before looping back to the south under the forested canopy. Cross Mission Dam and continue parallel to the creek. (The Pritchett Trail is a hillside loop to the west.) Campbell Bridge crosses the creek to the left, returning to the entrance. For a longer hike, continue south to the island section. The Easton-Aqueduct Trail loops around the hillside and descends to the creek at Stone Creek Crossing. Once across, head up the rock steps into the Manzanita Section, and return to the garden entrance.

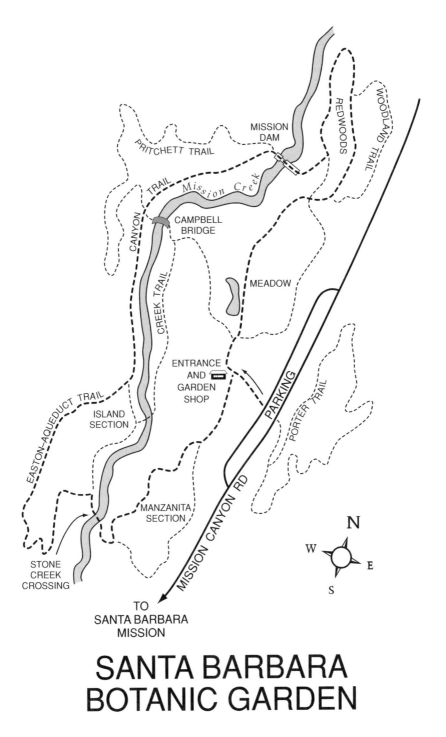

MISSION
DAM

PRITCHETT TRAIL

REDWOODS

WOODLAND TRAIL

TRAIL

Mission Creek

CANYON

CAMPBELL
BRIDGE

MEADOW

CREEK TRAIL

ENTRANCE
AND
GARDEN
SHOP

PARKING

PORTER TRAIL

EASTON-AQUEDUCT TRAIL

ISLAND
SECTION

MANZANITA
SECTION

MISSION CANYON RD

STONE
CREEK
CROSSING

N

W   E

S

TO
SANTA BARBARA
MISSION

SANTA BARBARA
BOTANIC GARDEN

Hike 13
Tunnel Fire Road

Hiking distance: 5.6 miles round trip
Hiking time: 2.5 hours
Elevation gain: 1,300 feet
Maps: Santa Barbara Front Country Recreational Map
U.S.G.S. Santa Barbara

Summary of hike: The Tunnel Fire Road is a utility easement road sometimes referred to as the Edison Catwalk. The trail is a steady, but not steep, uphill climb following the contours of the hillside. The hike leads to a hilltop overlook of Rattlesnake Canyon and offers great views of Santa Barbara and the Channel Islands.

Driving directions: From the Santa Barbara Mission, take Mission Canyon Road north towards the mountains for 0.6 miles to Foothill Road—turn right. Drive 0.2 miles to Mission Canyon Road and turn left. Continue 0.3 miles and bear left at a road split onto Tunnel Road. Drive 1.1 mile and park along the right side of the road near the road's end.

Hiking directions: Hike to the end of Tunnel Road and past the gate. Head uphill, winding around the hillside with great views of the city and ocean below. At 0.7 miles, the trail crosses a bridge over Mission Creek and Little Fern Canyon Falls (cover photo), arriving at a trail split where the paved trail ends. Bear to the right, staying on the unpaved road as it gains elevation along the contours of the hills. At 1.4 miles, there is a junction on the left with a connector trail to the Tunnel Trail. Stay to the right, entering a shady, forested area. The grade gets steeper as you near the top. The trail ends on the hilltop by utility poles overlooking Rattlesnake Canyon. To return, reverse your route.

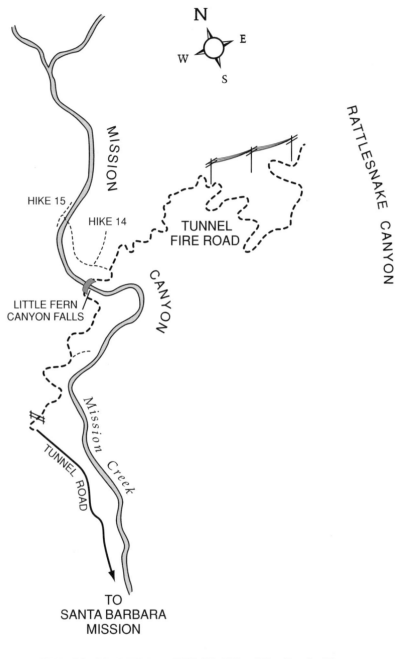

N

W E

S

MISSION

RATTLESNAKE CANYON

HIKE 15

HIKE 14

TUNNEL
FIRE ROAD

CANYON

LITTLE FERN
CANYON FALLS

Mission Creek

TUNNEL ROAD

TO
SANTA BARBARA
MISSION

TUNNEL FIRE ROAD

Hike 14
Tunnel Trail to Mission Falls

Hiking distance: 5.8 miles round trip
Hiking time: 3 hours
Elevation gain: 1,800 feet
Maps: Santa Barbara Front Country Recreational Map
       U.S.G.S. Santa Barbara

Summary of hike: The Tunnel Trail is named for a diversion tunnel built at the turn of the century that brings fresh water to Santa Barbara. The hike passes beautiful, weathered sandstone outcroppings on the way to panoramic views of Santa Barbara and the Channel Islands. The Tunnel Trail climbs along the eastern wall of Mission Canyon to an overlook atop the 200-foot Mission Falls. From the overlook, it is 1.2 miles further to East Camino Cielo Road.

Driving directions: To arrive at the trailhead, follow the driving directions for Hike 13.

Hiking directions: Head up Tunnel Road and past the trailhead gate. Continue up the curving road past Mission Creek. A bridge crosses the creek over Little Fern Canyon Falls (cover photo). At 0.7 miles, the paved road ends at a three-way junction. Take the left fork—the Jesusita Trail—for 150 yards to the Tunnel Trail junction on the right. Take this footpath through the brush to a junction with a service road at 1.2 miles. Cross the road, picking up the trail again. The steady, uphill trail passes the signed Rattlesnake Canyon Connector Trail at 2.3 miles on the right—stay left. Mission Falls can be seen across the canyon just before reaching this junction. Continue 0.7 miles to the creek crossing above the falls. Although it is a difficult scramble to see the falls up close, you will be able to sit among the large sandstone boulders above the falls and marvel at the views. Return along the same route.

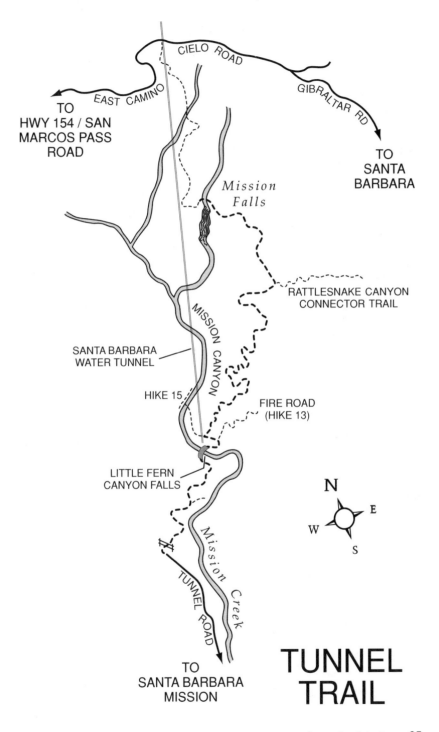

CIELO ROAD

EAST CAMINO

GIBRALTAR RD

TO
HWY 154 / SAN
MARCOS PASS
ROAD

TO
SANTA
BARBARA

Mission Falls

RATTLESNAKE CANYON
CONNECTOR TRAIL

MISSION CANYON

SANTA BARBARA
WATER TUNNEL

HIKE 15

FIRE ROAD
(HIKE 13)

LITTLE FERN
CANYON FALLS

N
E
W
S

Mission Creek

TUNNEL ROAD

TO
SANTA BARBARA
MISSION

TUNNEL
TRAIL

Hike 15
Seven Falls

Hiking distance: 2.5 miles round trip
Hiking time: 1.5 hours
Elevation gain: 600 feet
Maps: Santa Barbara Front Country Recreational Map
U.S.G.S. Santa Barbara

Summary of hike: Seven Falls is in a beautiful, sculpted gorge in Mission Canyon. Mission Creek cascades down the canyon and over boulders, creating more than a dozen waterfalls. The waterfalls drop into bowls etched into the sandstone rock, forming deep, rock-rimmed pools (back cover photo). One mile beyond Seven Falls is Inspiration Point, a scenic overlook.

Driving directions: To arrive at the trailhead, follow the driving directions for Hike 13.

Hiking directions: Hike up Tunnel Road and past the gate, following the paved road. The road splits at a half mile. Bear to the left, continuing uphill to a wooden bridge and waterfall. Cross the bridge over Mission Creek and Little Fern Canyon Falls (cover photo). At 0.7 miles, the pavement ends at another trail split and the trailhead kiosk. The right fork is a fire road (Hike 13). Take the left fork—the Jesusita Trail—into Mission Canyon. The trail descends into the forest to Mission Creek. Once across the creek, leave the Jesusita Trail, which leads to Inspiration Point. Instead, take the narrow path to the right up the west side of the canyon and parallel to the creek. Be careful! This is not a maintained trail and can be very tricky. Boulder climbing and branch dodging is involved as you slowly work your way up the narrow gorge past an endless display of waterfalls, cascades, and pools. Choose you own swimming hole and turnaround spot. There are additional waterfalls and pools down canyon from the main trail.

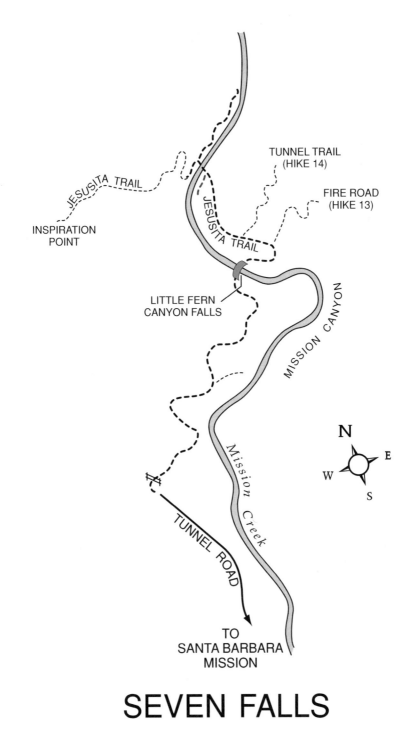

TUNNEL TRAIL
(HIKE 14)

FIRE ROAD
(HIKE 13)

JESUSITA TRAIL

JESUSITA TRAIL

INSPIRATION
POINT

LITTLE FERN
CANYON FALLS

MISSION CANYON

Mission Creek

N
E
W
S

TUNNEL ROAD

TO
SANTA BARBARA
MISSION

SEVEN FALLS

Hike 16
Jesusita Trail

Hiking distance: 3 miles round trip
Hiking time: 1.5 hours
Elevation gain: 700 feet
Maps: Santa Barbara Front Country Recreational Map
U.S.G.S. Santa Barbara

Summary of hike: The Jesusita Trail parallels San Roque Creek through a lush oak, sycamore, cottonwood, and willow woodland. The trail follows an easy course while crisscrossing the creek several times. The path leads up to a grassy meadow with scenic views of the surrounding area.

Driving directions: From Highway 101 in Santa Barbara, exit on Las Positas Road. Drive 2 miles north to the posted trailhead parking area on the left, just beyond the filtration plant. En route, Las Positas Road becomes San Roque Road after crossing State Street.

Hiking directions: From the parking area, head north past the trailhead sign. Within minutes is a junction. The left fork is a spur trail to the creek. Stay on the main trail while slowly dropping to the canyon bottom. Rock hop across the San Roque Creek and cross it again sixty feet ahead. Climb the steps and continue along the trail beside an avocado orchard on the right. The trail heads up canyon, parallel to the creek, while crossing several small tributary streams. At 0.7 miles, the trail leaves the creek to a grassy plateau. Descend back into the forest, and cross to the west side of the creek at one mile. There are three more crossings in quick succession as the trail passes a ranch. At the last crossing, the trail joins a dirt road at the Moreno Ranch entrance. This is the turnaround spot.

To hike further, the trail leaves the creek and heads east for two miles to Inspiration Point and Seven Falls (Hike 15).

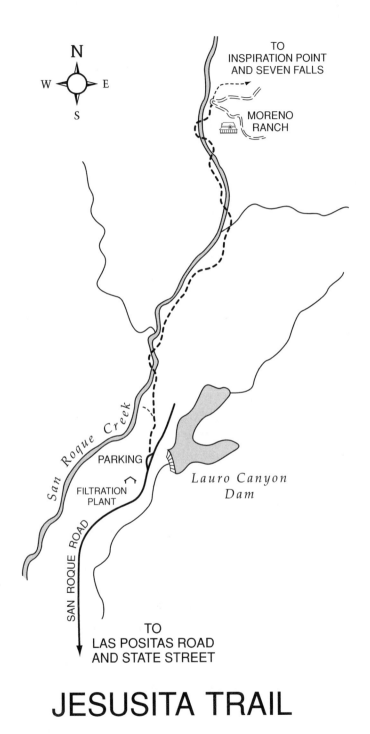

TO
INSPIRATION POINT
AND SEVEN FALLS

MORENO
RANCH

N
W   E
S

San Roque Creek

PARKING

FILTRATION
PLANT

SAN ROQUE ROAD

Lauro Canyon
Dam

TO
LAS POSITAS ROAD
AND STATE STREET

JESUSITA TRAIL

Hike 17
Las Positas Friendship Park
The Sierra Club Trail

Hiking distance: 1.3-mile loop
Hiking time: 40 minutes
Elevation gain: 300 feet
Maps: The Thomas Guide—Santa Barbara & Vicinity
U.S.G.S. Santa Barbara

Summary of hike: The Las Positas Friendship Park is a 236-acre hilltop park with a developed north side that includes baseball and soccer fields, gazebos, picnic areas, a war memorial, and an amphitheater. The natural south side of the park has nature trails leading up to a ridge overlooking Santa Barbara. There are surrounding views of the ocean harbor, the Channel Islands, and the Santa Ynez Mountains.

Driving directions: From Highway 101 in Santa Barbara, exit on Las Positas Road. Drive 1.2 miles south (toward the ocean) to the Las Positas Park entrance on the left at 1298 Las Positas Road. Take the park road—Jerry Harwin Parkway—0.4 miles to the signed trailhead on the right across from the soccer fields. Park in the lots on the left or straight ahead.

Hiking directions: Cross the park road to the signed trailhead and a junction. Take the right fork up a series of switchbacks. Various side paths may be confusing, but all the trails lead up to the hilltop perch overlooking South Park and Jesuit Hill. At the top, the 360-degree views are stunning. The Sierra Club Trail follows the ridge to the east before sharply curving back to the west. This begins the winding descent, completing the loop back at the trailhead. A steep, direct route leads down the center of the hill between the switchbacks.

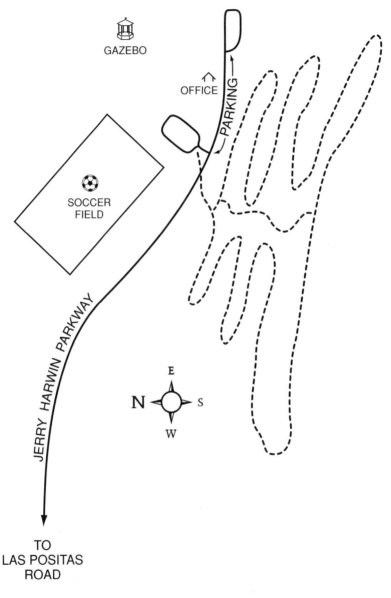

GAZEBO

OFFICE

PARKING →

SOCCER
FIELD

JERRY HARWIN PARKWAY

E

N → S

W

TO
LAS POSITAS
ROAD

LAS POSITAS
FRIENDSHIP PARK

Hike 18
Santa Barbara Coastal Bluffs

Hiking distance: 1.5 miles round trip
Hiking time: 1 hour
Elevation gain: 200 feet
Maps: The Thomas Guide—Santa Barbara & Vicinity
U.S.G.S. Santa Barbara

Summary of hike: The Santa Barbara Coastal Bluffs, also known as The Douglas Family Preserve, is a 70-acre grassy mesa with over 2,200 feet of rare, undeveloped ocean frontage. The preserve is covered with mature oaks, eucalyptus, and cypress trees. The trail loops around the mesa along the edge of the cliffs. Below the cliffs is the picturesque Arroyo Burro Beach, locally known as Hendry's Beach. There are picnic areas and a paved biking and walking path.

Driving directions: From Highway 101 in Santa Barbara, exit on Las Positas Road. Head 1.8 miles south (towards the ocean) to Cliff Drive and turn right. Continue 0.2 miles to the Arroyo Burro Beach parking lot on the left and park.

Hiking directions: From the parking lot, walk east on Cliff Drive to Las Positas Road. From here, a trail heads south past a chained gate into the forest. The trail curves left through the shady canopy up the hill. At the top, the trail levels out. Continue south along the eastern edge of the open space. Along the way several paths intersect from the right and several access trails come in from the left. At the bluffs overlooking the ocean, head west along the cliffs. At the west end of the cliffs is an overlook of Arroyo Burro Beach. The trail curves to the right and loops back to a junction at the top of the hill. Take a left, retracing your steps down the hill and back to the parking lot.

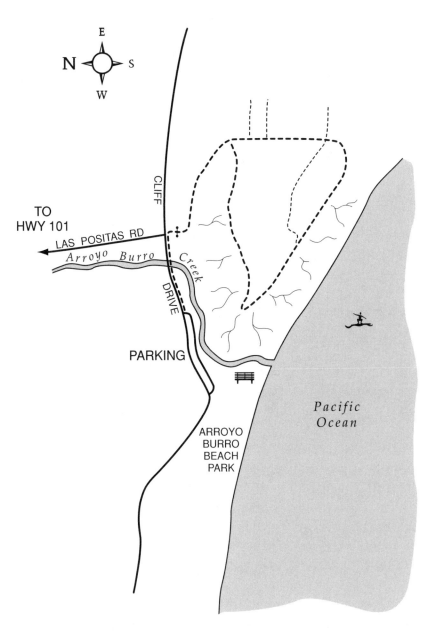

SANTA BARBARA
COASTAL BLUFFS

Hike 19
San Antonio Creek Trail

Hiking distance: 3.4 miles round trip
Hiking time: 1.5 hours
Elevation gain: 200 feet
Maps: Santa Barbara Front Country Recreational Map
U.S.G.S. Goleta

Summary of hike: The San Antonio Creek Trail begins at the far end of Tuckers Grove County Park in Goleta. The level trail follows San Antonio Canyon along the watercourse of the creek through grassy meadows and a shady woodland of bay laurel, oak, and sycamore trees.

Driving directions: From Santa Barbara, drive northbound on Highway 101, and exit on Turnpike Road in Goleta. Drive 0.6 miles north to Cathedral Oaks Road. Drive straight through the intersection, entering Tuckers Grove Park. Bear to the right through the parking lot, and drive 0.3 miles to the last parking area.

Hiking directions: From the parking lot, hike up the road and past the upper picnic ground, Kiwanis Meadow. Cross through the opening in the log fence to the left, heading towards the creek. Take the trail upstream along the east side of San Antonio Creek. Numerous spur trails lead down to the creek. At one mile, rock hop across the creek, and continue to a second crossing located between steep canyon walls. After crossing, the trail ascends a hill to a bench near a concrete flood-control dam. Head left across the top of the dam. The trail proceeds to the right, upstream, and recrosses San Antonio Creek. The forested canyon trail passes alongside a chain-link fence on the east side of the stream. The trail ends at 1.7 miles under a bridge where the trail intersects with Highway 154. Return along the same trail.

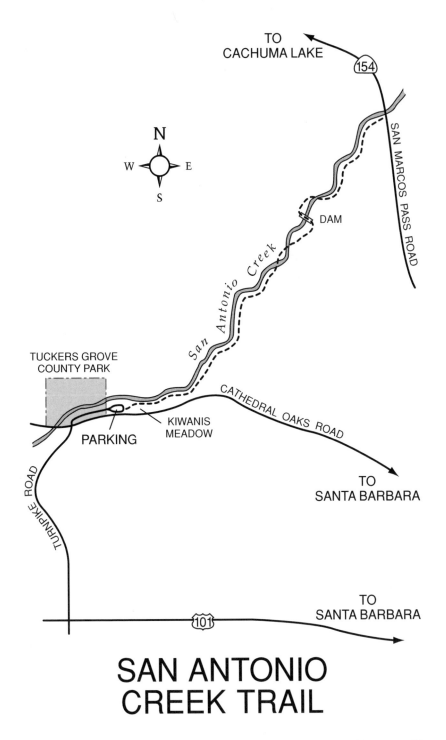

SAN ANTONIO
CREEK TRAIL

Hike 20
Goleta Beach and the UCSB Lagoon

Hiking distance: 4 miles round trip
Hiking time: 2 hours
Elevation gain: 50 feet
Maps: The Thomas Guide—Santa Barbara & Vicinity
U.S.G.S. Goleta

Summary of hike: This trail begins at Goleta Beach County Park and follows the coastal cliffs into the University of California—Santa Barbara. The trail circles the UCSB Lagoon to Goleta Point. The ocean surrounds the point on three sides, where there are tidepools and a beautiful coastline.

Driving directions: From Highway 101 in Goleta, exit onto Ward Memorial Boulevard/Highway 217. Continue 2 miles to the Sandspit Road exit, and turn left at the stop sign, heading towards Goleta Beach Park. Drive 0.3 miles to the beach parking lot turnoff. Turn right and cross the lagoon into the parking lot.

Hiking directions: Hike west along the park lawn to the bluffs overlooking the ocean. Continue past the natural bridge. The path parallels the cliff edge into the university. At the marine laboratory, take the right fork, crossing the road to the UCSB Lagoon. The lagoon sits on Goleta Point. Take the path to the right around the northeast side of the lagoon. At the north end, the trail joins a walking path in the university. At the west end of the lagoon, the trail heads south on the return portion of the loop. Once back at the ocean, climb up the bluff to the left. Continue around the lagoon and descend the steps between the lagoon and the ocean. Complete the loop back at the marine laboratory and bluffs. Head east, back to Goleta Beach Park.

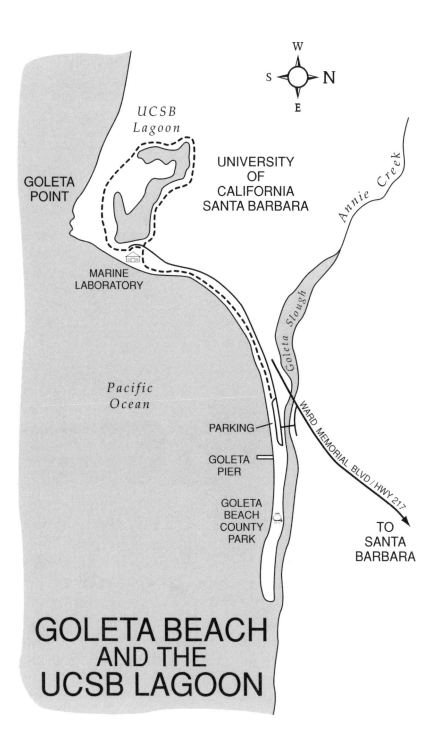

W
S ⊕ N
E

UCSB
Lagoon

UNIVERSITY
OF
CALIFORNIA
SANTA BARBARA

Annie Creek

GOLETA
POINT

Goleta Slough

MARINE
LABORATORY

*Pacific
Ocean*

PARKING

GOLETA
PIER

WARD MEMORIAL BLVD / HWY 217

GOLETA
BEACH
COUNTY
PARK

TO
SANTA
BARBARA

GOLETA BEACH
AND THE
UCSB LAGOON

Hike 21
Los Carneros County Park

Hiking distance: 1.5-mile loop
Hiking time: 1 hour
Elevation gain: Level
Maps: The Thomas Guide—Santa Barbara & Vicinity
      U.S.G.S. Goleta

Summary of hike: Los Carneros County Park is a nature preserve and bird habitat with a large lake. A network of trails meander across the park through rolling meadows and a forest of eucalyptus, oak, and pine trees. A wooden bridge crosses the northern end of the lake. At the trailhead is the Stow House, a Victorian home built in 1872, and the South Coast Railroad Museum, the original Goleta Train Station built in 1901. Both offer tours and exhibits.

Driving directions: From Santa Barbara, drive northbound on Highway 101 to Los Carneros Road in Goleta. Turn right and drive 0.3 miles north to the Stow House and Railroad Museum parking lot on the right. Turn right and park.

Hiking directions: From the parking lot, follow the rail fence past the Stow House. Continue straight ahead, following the sign to Los Carneros Lake and a junction. Take the paved path to the right. The path overlooks the lake. At the south end of the lake, a trail leads to the left and down to the lakeshore. Follow the shoreline around the southern end of the lake before heading up along the lake's east side. As you head north, the Santa Ynez Mountains are in full view. A variety of trails loop around the park, intersecting with each other. As you approach the north end of the lake, cross a wooden bridge over the willow and reed wetland. After crossing, the trail leads to the paved road near the trailhead. Head to the right, back to the parking lot.

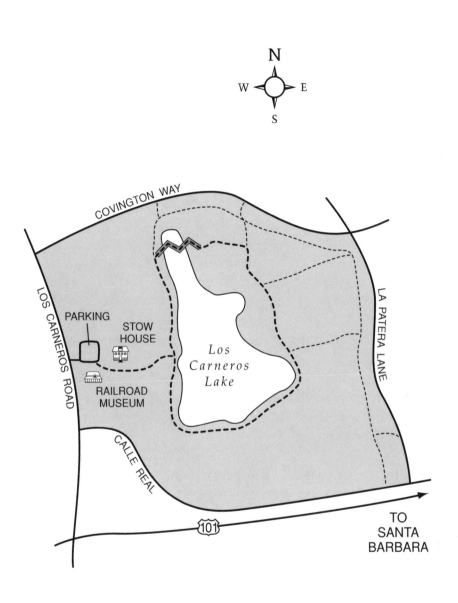

LOS CARNEROS
COUNTY PARK

Hike 22
Santa Barbara Shores
Ellwood Bluffs Trail

Hiking distance: 3.5 miles round trip
Hiking time: 1.5 hours
Elevation gain: Level
Maps: Santa Barbara County Recreational Map Series #8
U.S.G.S. Dos Pueblos Canyon

Summary of hike: Santa Barbara Shores County Park has a network of interconnecting trails across flat grasslands overlooking the Pacific Ocean. The Ellwood Bluffs Trail parallels 80-foot high cliffs along the ocean's edge. The eucalyptus groves are home to monarch butterflies during the winter months.

Driving directions: From Santa Barbara, drive northbound on Highway 101 to the Glen Annie Road/Storke Road exit in Goleta. Turn left on Storke Road, and drive 0.3 miles to Hollister Avenue, the first intersection. Turn right and continue 1.7 miles to the Santa Barbara County Park parking lot on the left, just past Ellwood School.

Hiking directions: At the trailhead is a junction. Take the right fork along the western edge of the parkland. The trail parallels a row of mature eucalyptus trees separating the Santa Barbara Shores County Park from the Sandpiper Golf Course. Continue south to the bluffs overlooking the ocean. Follow the trail to the left along the cliff's edge. Several trails cut across the open space to the left, returning to the trailhead for a shorter hike. At 0.5 miles is a junction with a beach access trail heading down to the mile-long beach. Further along the bluffs, take the trail inland, heading north along a row of eucalyptus trees. As you approach the eucalyptus groves, return along the prominent footpath to the left. The trail returns to the trailhead on the edge of the open meadows next to the groves.

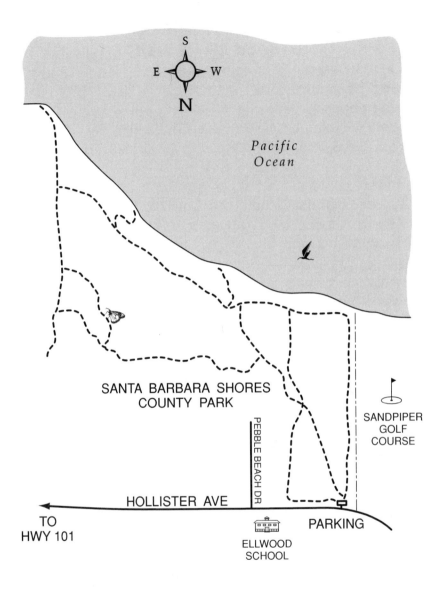

Pacific
Ocean

S
E · W
N

SANTA BARBARA SHORES
COUNTY PARK

SANDPIPER
GOLF
COURSE

PEBBLE BEACH DR

HOLLISTER AVE

TO
HWY 101

ELLWOOD
SCHOOL

PARKING

SANTA BARBARA SHORES
ELLWOOD BLUFFS TRAIL

Hike 23
El Capitan State Beach

Hiking distance: 1.5 miles round trip
Hiking time: 1 hour
Elevation gain: Level
Maps: El Capitan and Refugio State Beach—Park Service Map
U.S.G.S. Tajiguas

Summary of hike: Located west of Santa Barbara, El Capitan State Beach has a beautiful sandy beach with rocky tidepools. El Capitan Creek flows through a forested canyon to the tidepools. Nature trails weave through stands of sycamore and oak trees alongside the creek.

Driving directions: From Santa Barbara, drive 20 miles northbound on Highway 101 to the El Capitan State Beach exit. It is located 0.8 miles past the El Capitan Ranch Road exit. Turn left (south) and drive 0.3 miles to the state park entrance. Park in the day-use lot straight ahead.

Hiking directions: For a short walk, take the paved path that leads down the hillside from the general store to the ocean-front. The quarter-mile paved trail follows the shoreline a short distance to the east before looping back to the parking lot.
　　For a longer hike, continue along the shore on the unpaved path past a grassy picnic area to El Capitan Creek. Near the mouth of the creek are the tidepools. Take the "Nature Trail" footpath, heading inland through the woodlands while following El Capitan Creek upstream. You will pass several intersecting trails that loop back to the park entrance station and parking lot. Near the entrance station, pick up the trail on the west side of the road. The trail parallels the western edge of El Capitan Creek through the forested canyon. The trail ends at a railroad bridge where the trail meets the road. Return by reversing your route.

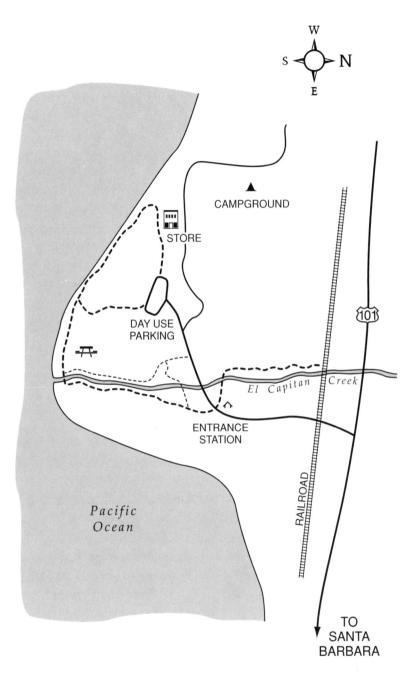

EL CAPITAN STATE BEACH

Hike 24
Gaviota Trail

Hiking distance: 3 miles round trip
Hiking time: 1.5 hours
Elevation gain: 750 feet
Maps: U.S.G.S. Gaviota

Summary of hike: The Gaviota Trail in Gaviota State Park leads to several scenic overlooks of the Pacific Ocean and Gaviota Peak. Along the way, the trail passes massive sandstone formations and caves.

Driving directions: From Santa Barbara, drive 33 miles northbound on Highway 101 to the Gaviota State Beach turnoff on the left. Turn left and drive 0.4 miles, bearing right near the entrance kiosk. Drive uphill to the trailhead parking area on the right.

Hiking directions: Head north past the locked gate on the paved road. The half-mile road leads through dense scrub bushes. A hundred yards before the road ends is the signed Multi-Purpose Trail on the left. Take this footpath up the south-facing hillside of the canyon. On the way up, views open up to the Pacific Ocean and Gaviota Peak. The trail steadily zigzags up to a ridge. At one mile the trail levels out near large, sculpted sandstone outcroppings and caves. Begin a second ascent to the largest formation, and curve around to the back side of the outcropping. Cross a ravine and continue uphill to the top to a junction with an old road. The left fork heads north into a valley and exits at Las Cruces near Highway 1 by the Las Cruces Adobe. Take the right fork a half mile to an overlook at the radio tower. Return by retracing your steps.

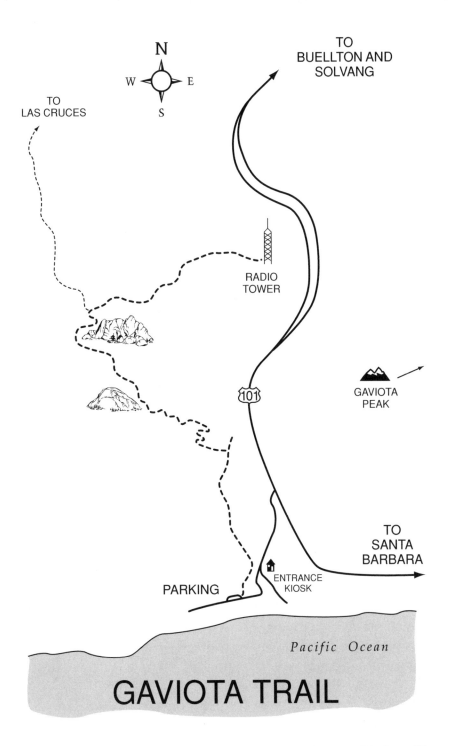

N

W E

S

TO
LAS CRUCES

TO
BUELLTON AND
SOLVANG

RADIO
TOWER

101

GAVIOTA
PEAK

TO
SANTA
BARBARA

PARKING

ENTRANCE
KIOSK

Pacific Ocean

GAVIOTA TRAIL

Hike 25
Gaviota Peak

Hiking distance: 6 miles round trip
Hiking time: 3 hours
Elevation gain: 1,900 feet
Maps: U.S.G.S. Solvang and Gaviota

Summary of hike: The trail to Gaviota Peak begins in Gaviota State Park and ends in the Los Padres National Forest. The trail passes Gaviota Hot Springs, a series of lukewarm, primitive sulphur spring pools that are popular for soaking. The hike to the peak is a substantial workout, but the views of the Santa Ynez Mountains, Lompoc Valley, the Pacific Ocean, and the Channel Islands are spectacular.

Driving directions: From Santa Barbara, drive 35 miles northbound on Highway 101 to the Highway 1 and Lompoc/Vandenberg AFB exit. Turn sharply to the right onto the frontage road, and continue 0.3 miles to the Gaviota State Park parking lot at the road's end.

Hiking directions: Hike east past the trailhead on the wide, unpaved road under the shade of oak and sycamore trees. Stay on the main trail past a junction with the Trespass Trail. Cross a stream to a junction at 0.4 miles. The right fork is a short side trip to Gaviota Hot Springs. After enjoying the springs, return to the junction and continue on the left fork, following the old road as it curves around the grassy hillside. From here, there are views of the rolling hills and ranches of the Lompoc Valley. Long, gradual switchbacks lead up to the national forest boundary at 1.5 miles. At two miles, the trail reaches a saddle with more great views. The grade of the trail is never steep, but it rarely levels out. Near the top, pass a metal gate to a junction. Take the right fork for the final ascent to the peak and the spectacular views. Return along the same trail.

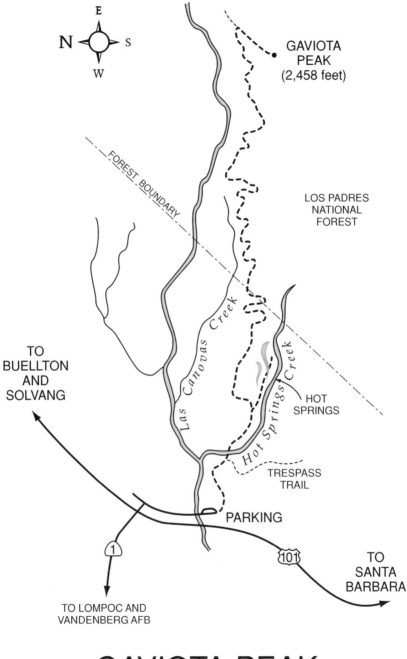

E
N ← ☉ → S
W

GAVIOTA
PEAK
(2,458 feet)

FOREST BOUNDARY

LOS PADRES
NATIONAL
FOREST

Las Canovas Creek

Hot Springs Creek

HOT
SPRINGS

TO
BUELLTON
AND
SOLVANG

TRESPASS
TRAIL

PARKING

1

101

TO
SANTA
BARBARA

TO LOMPOC AND
VANDENBERG AFB

GAVIOTA PEAK

Hike 26
Nojoqui Falls

Hiking distance: 0.6 miles round trip
Hiking time: 30 minutes
Elevation gain: 50 feet
Maps: U.S.G.S. Solvang

Summary of hike: Nojoqui Falls is located in a cool, north facing canyon in the grassy Nojoqui Falls County Park. The waterfall cascades 80 feet down a mossy, fern-covered rock wall and into a pool. The well-maintained trail to the falls winds through a shady glen under oaks, bays, laurels, and sycamores. The trail crosses three wooden bridges over a year-round creek on the way to the pool and grotto at the base of the falls.

Driving directions: From Santa Barbara, drive 38 miles northbound on Highway 101. Turn right at the Nojoqui Falls Park sign on the Old Coast Highway. The turnoff is located 3.6 miles past the Highway 1 exit. Drive one mile to Alisal Road. Turn left and continue 0.8 miles to the Nojoqui Falls Park entrance on the right. Turn right and drive straight ahead to the last parking lot. If full, park in the first parking area.
Heading south on Highway 101, the Nojoqui Falls Park turnoff is 4.1 miles south of the Santa Rosa Road exit, the southernmost exit of Buellton.

Hiking directions: Hike to the trailhead at the south end of the second parking area. The wide path parallels Nojoqui Creek as it cascades down canyon. A series of three bridge crossings lead to the base of the falls below the sandstone cliffs. Relax on the large rock slabs and benches at the trail's end while viewing the falls.

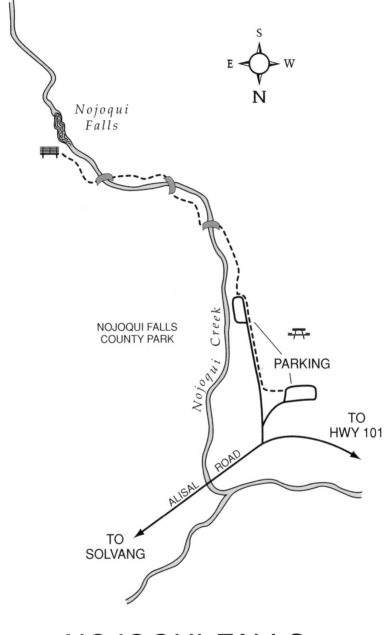

Nojoqui Falls

NOJOQUI FALLS COUNTY PARK

Nojoqui Creek

PARKING

TO HWY 101

ALISAL ROAD

TO SOLVANG

NOJOQUI FALLS

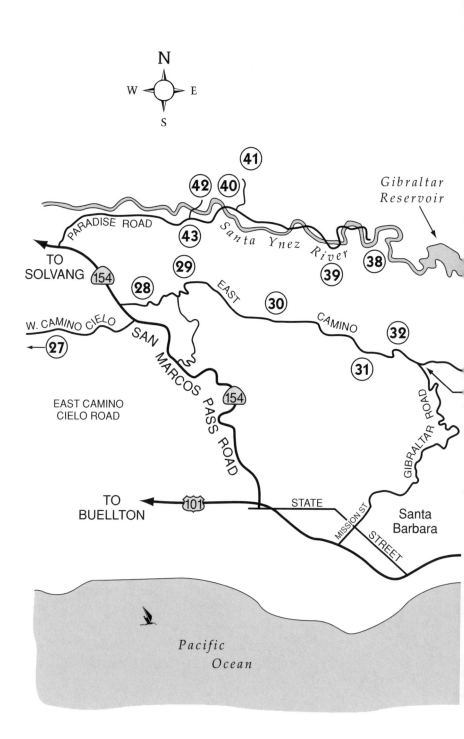

N

W E

S

(41)

(42) (40)

Gibraltar
Reservoir

PARADISE ROAD

(43)

Santa Ynez River

TO
SOLVANG (154)

(38)

(29)

(39)

(28)

EAST

(30)

W. CAMINO CIELO

SAN MARCOS PASS ROAD

CAMINO

(32)

(27)

(31)

EAST CAMINO
CIELO ROAD

(154)

GIBRALTAR ROAD

TO
BUELLTON

(101)

STATE

MISSION ST

STREET

Santa
Barbara

Pacific
Ocean

THE UPPER COUNTRY
HIKES 27 –43
Camino Cielo Road and
the Santa Ynez River Valley

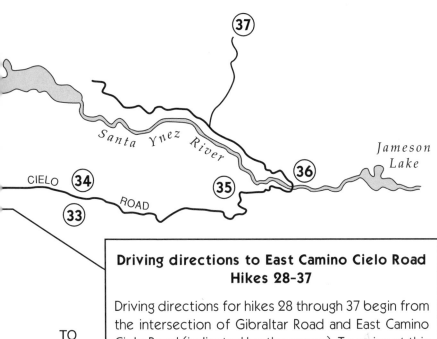

Driving directions to East Camino Cielo Road
Hikes 28-37

Driving directions for hikes 28 through 37 begin from the intersection of Gibraltar Road and East Camino Cielo Road (indicated by the arrow). To arrive at this intersection, follow these directions:

From the Santa Barbara Mission, take Mission Canyon Road north towards the mountains for 0.6 miles to Foothill Road—turn right. Drive 0.8 miles to West Mountain Drive and turn left. Continue 0.4 miles, bearing left at a road split while staying on West Mountain Drive. Continue 0.2 miles to Gibraltar Road and bear to the right. Begin winding and climbing for 6.5 miles up the mountain road to East Camino Cielo Road.

Hike 27
Lizard's Mouth

Hiking distance: 0.5 to 1 mile round trip
Hiking time: 30 minutes
Elevation gain: 100 feet
Maps: Santa Barbara Front Country map
U.S.G.S. San Marcos Pass and Goleta

Summary of hike: Lizard's Mouth, named for a specific weatherworn formation, is an area with huge rock slabs, sculpted sandstone outcroppings, and a variety of caves and crevices. The dramatic landscape is perched on the south-facing, chaparral-covered slopes of the Santa Ynez Mountains overlooking Santa Barbara and the Pacific Ocean.

Driving directions: From Highway 101 in Santa Barbara, take the State Street/Highway 154 exit. Turn right on Highway 154 (San Marcos Pass Road), and drive 7 miles to West Camino Cielo Road on the left. Turn left and continue 3.8 miles to pullouts along both sides of the road. The unmarked trail is to the left (south). If you reach the Winchester Gun Club entrance on the left, you have gone about 100 yards past the trailhead.

Hiking directions: From the parking pullout, hike south through the chaparral for a short 200 feet to a clearing at the unique rock formations. Several other unmarked paths also lead south through the brush to these formations. Once at the outcroppings, pick your own trail to the numerous overlooks, caves, and crevices. The trails do not lead anywhere specific. They just meander across the giant slabs of rock among the primeval looking sandstone and boulders.

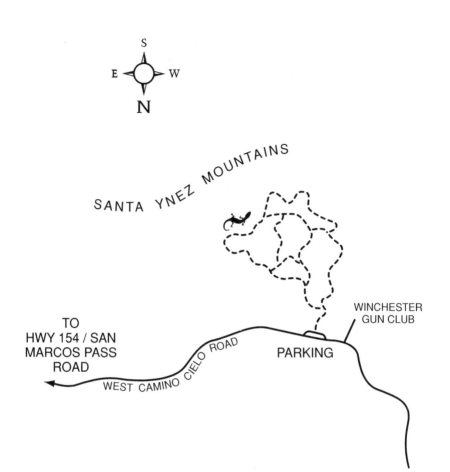

S

E W

N

SANTA YNEZ MOUNTAINS

WINCHESTER
GUN CLUB

TO
HWY 154 / SAN
MARCOS PASS
ROAD

WEST CAMINO CIELO ROAD

PARKING

BRUSH PEAK
(3,069 feet)

LIZARD'S MOUTH

Hike 28
Fremont Trail

Hiking distance: 4 miles round trip
Hiking time: 2 hours
Elevation gain: 800 feet
Maps: Santa Barbara Front Country Recreational Map
U.S.G.S. San Marcos Pass

Summary of hike: The Fremont Trail is a restricted vehicle road that winds down towards the Santa Ynez Valley past sandstone formations and a series of knolls. The hike has great views from Santa Barbara's mountainous interior of Cachuma Lake to the west, the national forest to the north, and the Pacific Ocean and Channel Islands to the south.

Driving directions: From Highway 101 in Santa Barbara, take the State Street/Highway 154 exit. Turn right on Highway 154 (San Marcos Pass Road), and drive 7.8 miles to East Camino Cielo Road on the right. Turn right and continue 1.6 miles to a closed Forest Service gate on the left. Parking pullouts are on the left past the trailhead gate.

Hiking directions: Hike past the Forest Service gate and head downhill. The trail follows the ridge that overlooks Los Laureles Canyon to the west and Paradise Canyon to the east. After the initial half-mile descent, the trail levels out. At one mile the trail begins a second descent and curves to the west. The trail reaches and passes under utility poles at two miles. This is a good turnaround point. Return along the same trail.

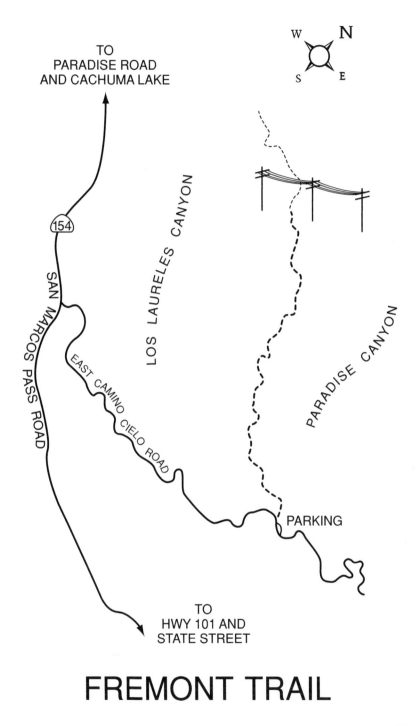

W **N**

S **E**

TO
PARADISE ROAD
AND CACHUMA LAKE

154

SAN MARCOS PASS ROAD

LOS LAURELES CANYON

EAST CAMINO CIELO ROAD

PARADISE CANYON

PARKING

TO
HWY 101 AND
STATE STREET

FREMONT TRAIL

Hike 29
Knapp's Castle
from East Camino Cielo Road

Hiking distance: 0.8 miles round trip
Hiking time: 30 minutes
Elevation gain: 100 feet
Maps: Santa Barbara Front Country Recreational Map
U.S.G.S. San Marcos Pass

Summary of hike: Knapp's Castle is a stone ruin that sits on a rocky point with stunning vistas. An easy half-mile hike from East Camino Cielo Road leads to the 1916 sandstone mansion. What remains is the foundation, rock arches, fireplaces, chimneys, and rock stairways. The rest was consumed in the 1940 Paradise Canyon Fire. The spectacular views extend up and down the Santa Ynez Valley from Gibraltar Dam to Cachuma Lake. Although the castle sits on private property, the current owner graciously allows access.

Driving directions: From Highway 101 in Santa Barbara, take the State Street/Highway 154 exit. Turn right on Highway 154 (San Marcos Pass Road), and drive 7.8 miles to East Camino Cielo Road on the right. Turn right and continue 3 miles to a closed Forest Service gate on the left. The gate is 0.9 miles past Painted Cave Road. Parking pullouts are on the right side of the road.

Hiking directions: Cross East Camino Cielo Road and hike north past the Forest Service "Private Property" gate. The trail, an unpaved road, crosses the hillside to a trail split at 0.4 miles. The left fork is the Snyder Trail, leading three miles down to Paradise Road in the Santa Ynez Valley (Hike 43). Bear to the right past a second "Private Property" gate. The ruins sit on a point overlooking the valley. After walking through the ruins and marveling at the views, return along the same path.

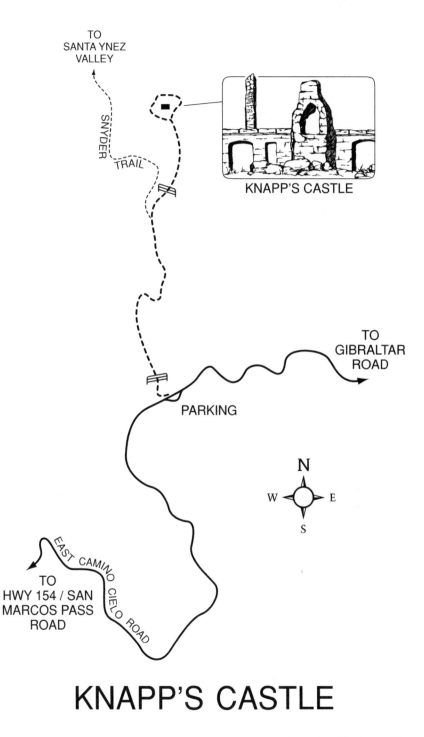

TO
SANTA YNEZ
VALLEY

SNYDER

TRAIL

KNAPP'S CASTLE

TO
GIBRALTAR
ROAD

PARKING

N

W ⊙ E

S

EAST CAMINO CIELO ROAD

TO
HWY 154 / SAN
MARCOS PASS
ROAD

KNAPP'S CASTLE

Hike 30
Arroyo Burro Trail

Hiking distance: 6.5 mile loop
Hiking time: 3.5 hours
Elevation gain: 1,700 feet
Maps: Santa Barbara Front Country Recreational Map
U.S.G.S. San Marcos Pass and Little Pine Mountain

Summary of hike: The Arroyo Burro Trail, originally a Chumash Indian route, leads down a narrow, rocky canyon with a year-round stream. The trail connects with the Arroyo Burro Road just south of White Oak Camp. The hike returns along the winding Arroyo Burro Road, an unpaved, vehicle-restricted road.

Driving directions: From the intersection of Gibraltar Road and East Camino Cielo Road, drive 4.9 miles west on East Camino Cielo Road to an unpaved road on the right. Turn right and head north 0.1 mile to a locked gate and parking pullouts.

From Highway 154 (San Marcos Pass Road), drive 6.2 miles east on East Camino Cielo Road to the turnoff.

Hiking directions: Hike north past the locked gate on the graded Arroyo Burro Road. A hundred yards past the gate is a signed junction for the Arroyo Burro Trail on the left. Leave the road and head downhill to the left on the footpath. This is the beginning of the loop, as you will return on the graded road. The trail quickly descends into the narrow Arroyo Burro Canyon and crosses a stream several times. At three miles, the trail rejoins the Arroyo Burro Road just above White Oak Camp. For the return, take the winding road along the east canyon wall back to the trailhead.

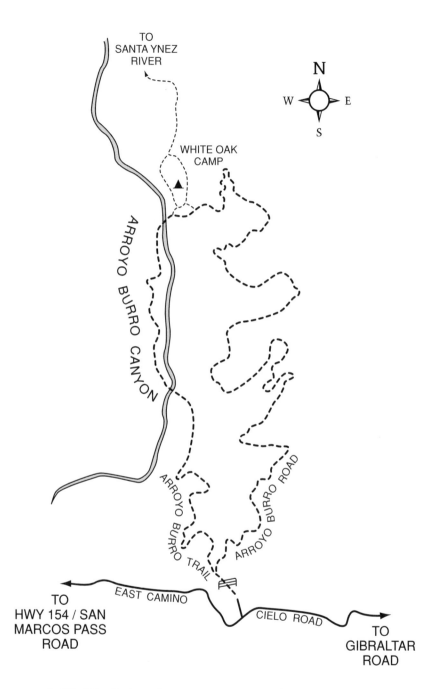

ARROYO BURRO TRAIL

Hike 31
La Cumbre Vista Point

Hiking distance: 0.3 to 0.8 miles round trip
Hiking time: 30 minutes
Elevation gain: 100 feet
Maps: U.S.G.S. Santa Barbara

Summary of hike: Although this is a short hike, it is a magical location and well worth the stop. The loop trail leads to La Cumbre Peak, a 3,985-foot panoramic overlook with incredible views. Cathedral Peak can be seen a short half mile to the south and 650 feet lower. The unobstructed views of Santa Barbara and the coastline are superb. On clear days, you can see all the way to Point Mugu in the Santa Monica Mountains.

Driving directions: From the intersection of Gibraltar Road and East Camino Cielo Road, drive 1.9 miles west on East Camino Cielo Road to the signed trailhead and parking pullouts on the left side.
From Highway 154 (San Marcos Pass Road), drive 9.2 miles east on East Camino Cielo Road.

Hiking directions: From the parking pullout, hike up the gated, asphalt road past the pine trees to a junction. Take the right fork and return on the left fork. At the first overlook is a bench. Footpaths lead down to large, sculpted boulders and additional overlooks. Continue on the winding road, heading east to a second overlook with benches. Again, footpaths lead downhill to more overlooks. The main trail loops around, passing a fenced satellite station, back to the trailhead.

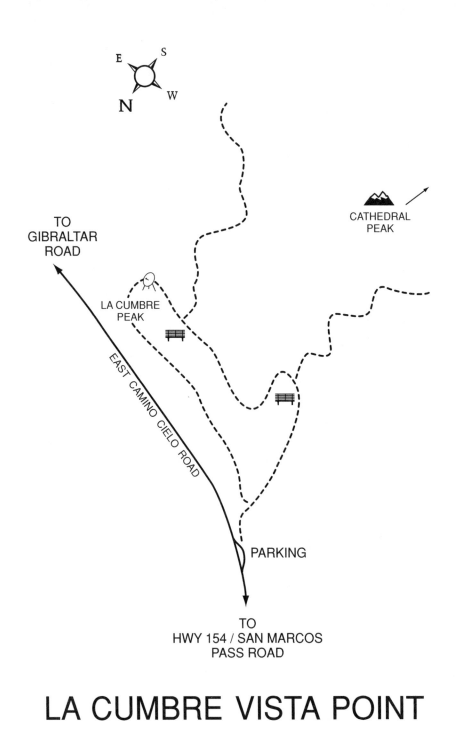

TO
GIBRALTAR
ROAD

CATHEDRAL
PEAK

LA CUMBRE
PEAK

EAST CAMINO CIELO ROAD

PARKING

TO
HWY 154 / SAN MARCOS
PASS ROAD

E   S

N   W

LA CUMBRE VISTA POINT

Hike 32
Angostura Pass Road

Hiking distance: 3 to 14 miles round trip
Hiking time: 1.5 to 7 hours
Elevation gain: 1,000 to 2,000 feet
Maps: Santa Barbara Front Country Recreational Map
U.S.G.S. Santa Barbara and Little Pine Mountain

Summary of hike: The Angostura Pass Road is a service road that leads seven miles down the north face of the Santa Ynez Mountains to Gibraltar Dam. The hike down the road overlooks Gibraltar Lake and Dam. There are great views across the Santa Ynez Valley of Little Pine and Big Pine Mountains. Along the way, the Matias Potrero Trail connects the Angostura Road with the Arroyo Burro Road to the northwest. The Matias Potrero Trail also connects with the Devils Canyon Trail that heads into Devils Canyon and down to Gibraltar Dam.

Driving directions: From the intersection of Gibraltar Road and East Camino Cielo Road, drive 0.7 miles west on East Camino Cielo Road to an unpaved road and parking pullout on the right.

From Highway 154 (San Marcos Pass Road), drive 10.4 miles east on East Camino Cielo Road.

Hiking directions: Take the graded road 100 yards north to the locked gate. Continue past the gate for about a mile to a signed junction with the steep Matias Potrero Trail, a footpath heading down to the left. Stay on the road as it heads east across the contours of the mountain. At two miles, the trail begins heading around Devils Canyon. As you look across the mountainside, the road can be seen winding its way down to Gibraltar Dam. Choose your own turnaround spot anywhere along the road.

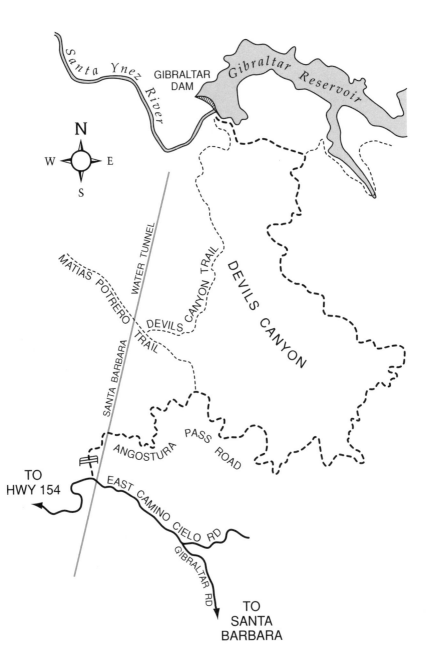

ANGOSTURA PASS ROAD

Hike 33
Montecito Peak

Hiking distance: 4 miles round trip
Hiking time: 2 hours
Elevation gain: 700 feet
Maps: Santa Barbara Front Country Recreational Map
U.S.G.S. Santa Barbara

Summary of hike: This hike leads to Montecito Peak, a bald, dome-shaped mountain with a 3,214-foot summit and a diameter of about 50 feet. There are magnificent 360-degree views of the coastal communities and the ocean. The hike begins at the top of the Santa Ynez Mountains on East Camino Cielo Road and descends 700 feet down the south face of the mountains. Montecito Peak can also be reached from the East Fork of Cold Spring Canyon (Hike 8).

Driving directions: From the intersection of Gibraltar Road and East Camino Cielo Road, drive 3.6 miles east on East Camino Cielo Road. The trailhead parking area is on the right side of the road by a large cement water tank.

Hiking directions: From the parking area, take the Cold Spring Trail heading south on the right side of the water tank. The well-defined path overlooks Santa Barbara, the ocean, and the Channel Islands as it heads downhill. The trail curves around the mountainside towards the prominent Montecito Peak. At 1.2 miles, the trail approaches the northwest side of the dome, then skirts around the western edge of the mountain, heading down to the East Fork of Cold Spring Canyon. As you first near the dome, watch for a narrow, steep, unmarked path on the left. Take this path to a ridge. From here, it is a short, but steep, 200-foot scramble to the summit. Careful footing is a must! Return on the same trail to the road and parking lot.

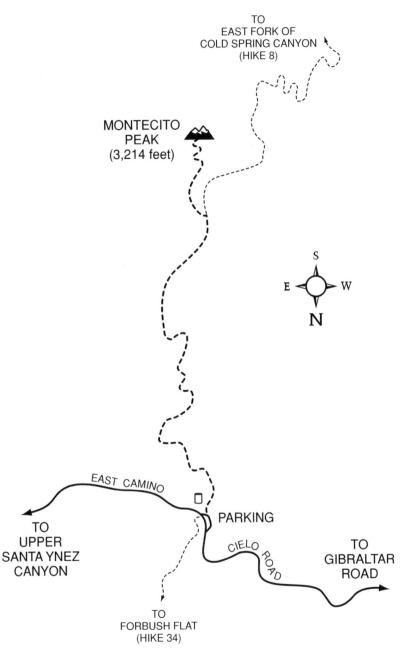

TO
EAST FORK OF
COLD SPRING CANYON
(HIKE 8)

MONTECITO
PEAK
(3,214 feet)

S

E — W

N

EAST CAMINO

TO
UPPER
SANTA YNEZ
CANYON

PARKING

CIELO ROAD

TO
GIBRALTAR
ROAD

TO
FORBUSH FLAT
(HIKE 34)

MONTECITO PEAK

Hike 34
Forbush Flat

Hiking distance: 4 miles round trip
Hiking time: 2.5 hours
Elevation gain: 1,000 feet
Maps: Santa Barbara Front Country Recreational Map
U.S.G.S. Santa Barbara

Summary of hike: This hike descends a thousand feet down the north slope of the Santa Ynez Mountains to Forbush Flat, a beautiful meadow located by Gidney Creek. Forbush Flat was the location of an old homestead from the early 1900s. The only remnant of the homestead is an aging fruit tree orchard. From the flat, the trail continues west down Forbush Canyon and north to the Santa Ynez River.

Driving directions: From the intersection of Gibraltar Road and East Camino Cielo Road, drive 3.6 miles east on East Camino Cielo Road. The trailhead parking area is on the right side of the road by a large cement water tank.

Hiking directions: Cross East Camino Cielo Road to the Cold Spring Trail. Head steeply downhill on the west side of the canyon. At 0.5 miles, after several switchbacks, the trail crosses a seasonal stream to a bench. Continue downhill along the chaparral-covered canyon wall. At one mile, the trail opens up to beautiful vistas of the Santa Ynez Valley and the mountains beyond. From here, look back up the canyon. When the creek is flowing, a 25-foot waterfall cascades off the rock wall. At two miles, the trail reaches Forbush Flat. The orchard, meadow, and campsites are on the left. The main trail continues a short distance down a series of switchbacks to Gidney Creek and a junction. The right fork leads two miles to Cottam Camp and Blue Canyon (Hike 35). Straight ahead, the trail leads two miles to the Santa Ynez River. To return, take the same trail back.

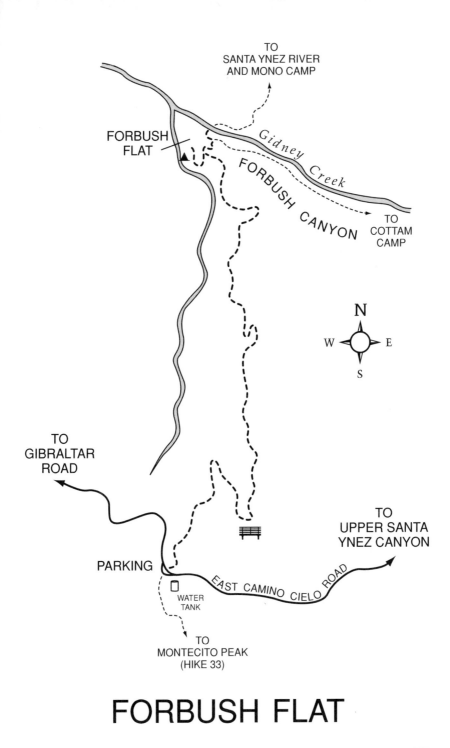

TO
SANTA YNEZ RIVER
AND MONO CAMP

FORBUSH
FLAT

Gidney Creek

FORBUSH CANYON

TO
COTTAM
CAMP

N
W — E
S

TO
GIBRALTAR
ROAD

TO
UPPER SANTA
YNEZ CANYON

PARKING

EAST CAMINO CIELO ROAD

WATER
TANK

TO
MONTECITO PEAK
(HIKE 33)

FORBUSH FLAT

Hike 35
Blue Canyon

Hiking distance: 3.2 miles round trip
Hiking time: 1.5 hours
Elevation gain: 200 feet
Maps: Santa Barbara Front Country Recreational Map
      U.S.G.S. Carpinteria

Summary of hike: The Blue Canyon Trail follows Escondido Creek through a narrow canyon past weathered sandstone outcroppings and blue-green serpentine rock. The lush canyon has stands of oak, sycamore, and alder trees. The trail leads to Upper Blue Canyon Camp, a primitive camp along the banks of a stream near pools and cascades.

Driving directions: From the intersection of Gibraltar Road and East Camino Cielo Road, drive 10.4 east miles on East Camino Cielo Road to the trailhead and parking pullout on the left.

Hiking directions: Hike west along the north canyon wall, immediately dropping into Blue Canyon. At 0.3 miles and again at 0.6 miles, the trail passes a series of beautifully eroded sandstone formations. The trail gradually descends to Escondido Creek and the forested canyon floor at one mile. Cross the creek and continue downstream to a stream crossing at 1.5 miles. Cross the stream to Upper Blue Canyon Camp on a small flat above the water. A short distance beyond the camp is another crossing of Escondido Creek. This is the turnaround spot.

To hike further, the trail continues through the canyon another 3.5 miles to Cottam Camp and 5.5 miles to Forbush Flat (Hike 34).

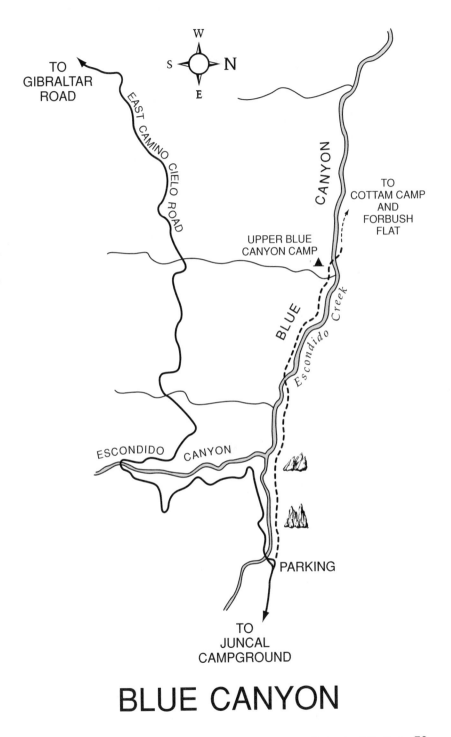

W N S E

TO
GIBRALTAR
ROAD

EAST CAMINO CIELO ROAD

CANYON

TO
COTTAM CAMP
AND
FORBUSH
FLAT

UPPER BLUE
CANYON CAMP ▲

BLUE

Escondido Creek

ESCONDIDO CANYON

PARKING

TO
JUNCAL
CAMPGROUND

BLUE CANYON

Hike 36
Jameson Lake

Hiking distance: 7 miles round trip
Hiking time: 3.5 hours
Elevation gain: 500 feet
Maps: Santa Barbara Front Country Recreational Map
U.S.G.S. Carpinteria and White Ledge Peak

Summary of hike: The hike to Jameson Lake heads up Juncal Canyon to the upper end of the Santa Ynez drainage. The trail follows the Santa Ynez River and parallels the south shore of the reservoir. There are great views down the Santa Ynez Valley to the west and to the upper canyon in the east.

Driving directions: From the intersection of Gibraltar Road and East Camino Cielo Road, drive 12 miles east on East Camino Cielo Road to the Juncal Campground at the bottom of the valley. Turn right, entering the campground, and continue straight ahead. Park at the far east end.

Hiking directions: At the far end of the Juncal Campground, head east past the gate on the unpaved Juncal Road. Cross the stream and follow the near-level road to the upper end of the canyon, parallel to the Santa Ynez River. The side trails lead down to the river. At 1.5 miles, cross the river spillway. After crossing, the trail begins an ascent, curving up and around the west side of the mountain. Views open up to the east and west, including the first look at Jameson Lake. As you round the mountain towards the south, the trail continues above Alder Creek and parallel to the south shore of Jameson Lake. At 3.5 miles is a junction on the right with the Alder Creek trail. This is the turnaround spot.

To hike further, the trail leads down to Alder Creek and follows the creek past pools and small waterfalls to Alder Camp, one mile ahead.

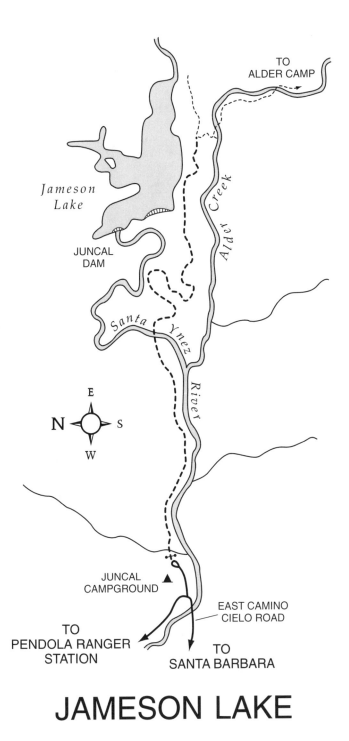

TO
ALDER CAMP

Jameson
Lake

Alder Creek

JUNCAL
DAM

Santa Ynez River

E
N S
W

JUNCAL
CAMPGROUND

EAST CAMINO
CIELO ROAD

TO
PENDOLA RANGER
STATION

TO
SANTA BARBARA

JAMESON LAKE

Hike 37
Agua Caliente Canyon

Hiking distance: 4 miles round trip
Hiking time: 2 hours
Elevation gain: 200 feet
Maps: Santa Barbara Front Country map
       Dick Smith Wilderness map
       U.S.G.S. Hildreth Peak

Summary of hike: Agua Caliente, meaning "hot water," is home to Big Caliente Hot Springs, a bathing pool near the trailhead that is perfect for soaking after the hike. The hike up Agua Caliente Canyon follows the creek along an old pack trail past Big Caliente Debris Dam. At the dam is an overlook of its 70-foot tall spillway.

Driving directions: From the intersection of Gibraltar Road and East Camino Cielo Road, drive 12 miles east on East Camino Cielo Road to the Juncal Campground at the bottom of the valley. Bear left and continue 3 miles to the Pendola Ranger Station at Big Caliente Road on the right. Turn right and drive 2.4 miles to Caliente Hot Springs. Park off the road.

Hiking directions: Follow the unpaved road up canyon past the cement hot springs pool. A short distance ahead, the road narrows to a footpath by a trail sign. The path parallels the creek past a series of pools. At 0.5 miles, the trail crosses the creek and heads gently uphill to the Big Caliente Dam and the spillway overlook. Past the dam, the trail levels out through a lush, forested flat, staying close to the watercourse. The trail recrosses the creek at 1.6 miles near the mouth of Diablo Canyon. Bear to the left, continuing deeper into Agua Caliente Canyon. At two miles the trail crosses the creek, and the canyon narrows. This is a good turnaround spot. To hike further, the trail continues for several miles up the canyon.

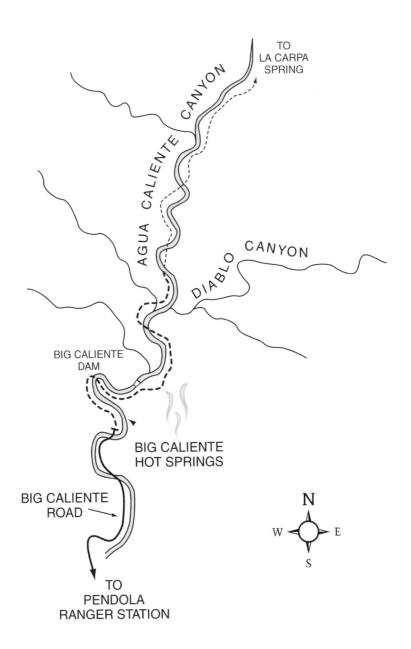

TO
LA CARPA
SPRING

AGUA CALIENTE CANYON

DIABLO CANYON

BIG CALIENTE
DAM

BIG CALIENTE
HOT SPRINGS

BIG CALIENTE
ROAD

N
W E
S

TO
PENDOLA
RANGER STATION

AGUA CALIENTE CANYON

Hike 38
Red Rocks to Gibraltar Dam

Hiking distance: 6.5 miles round trip
Hiking time: 3 hours
Elevation gain: 500 feet
Maps: Santa Barbara Front Country Map
       U.S.G.S. Little Pine Mountain

Summary of hike: The Red Rocks Trail follows the Santa Ynez River up the twisting canyon to Gibraltar Dam. Along the way there are numerous swimming holes and beautiful rock formations. Two routes lead to the dam, creating a loop hike. The Upper Road, known locally as the High Road, is a vehicle-restricted road that traverses the mountains overlooking the Santa Ynez River, the swimming holes, and the surrounding hills. The River Trail, once a mining road, winds along the canyon floor with frequent river crossings. The River Trail can be difficult and is not recommended during high water. At that time, return along the High Road.

Driving directions: From Highway 101 in Santa Barbara, take the State Street/Highway 154 exit. Turn right on Highway 154 (San Marcos Pass Road), and drive 10.6 miles to Paradise Road on the right. Turn right and continue 10.4 miles to the trailhead parking area on the left. It is located near the end of the road.

Hiking directions: The High Road begins at the end of Paradise Road at the locked gate. The road skirts along the contours of the mountain, gaining a quick 200 feet up switchbacks before leveling off on a plateau. At two miles are the first views of Gibraltar Dam. The trail descends from here, passing the Devil's Canyon Trail, to the junction with the River Trail. The right fork leads to the dam. The left fork leads to a swimming pool at the river and begins the return trip. The trail meanders down the forested canyon, frequently crossing the river back to the trailhead.

If you are here to cool off in a pool, take the River Trail (at the east end of the parking area) 0.3 miles to the popular Red Rocks swimming pool. Just before the pool is a trail split. The left fork is the main trail to Gibraltar Dam. The right fork leads down to the shoreline. Red rock cliffs tower over the pool.

DEVIL'S
CANYON
TRAIL

*Gibraltar
Reservoir*

GIBRALTAR
DAM

RIVER TRAIL

HIGH ROAD

E   S

N   W

PARKING

TO
HWY 154 / SAN
MARCOS PASS
ROAD

RED ROCKS
POOL

PARADISE RD

RED ROCKS
CAMPGROUND

Santa Ynez River

RED ROCKS
TO GIBRALTAR DAM

Hike 39
Matias Potrero Trail

Hiking distance: 3 miles round trip
Hiking time: 1.5 hours
Elevation gain: 600 feet
Maps: Santa Ynez Recreation Area map
Santa Barbara Front Country Recreational Map
U.S.G.S. Little Pine Mountain

Summary of hike: The Matias Potrero Trail is a connector trail between Arroyo Burro Trail and Angostura Pass Road (Hikes 30 and 32). The picturesque trail follows the Santa Ynez Fault along the grassy north slopes of the Santa Ynez Mountains, passing meadows, rolling hills, canyons, rock formations, and chaparral. The trail leads to Matias Potrero Camp, a primitive campsite in an oak grove with a picnic table and rock cookstove.

Driving directions: From Highway 101 in Santa Barbara, take the State Street/Highway 154 exit. Turn right on Highway 154 (San Marcos Pass Road), and drive 10.6 miles to Paradise Road on the right. Turn right and continue 9 miles to the parking area on the left, across the road from the signed trailhead.

Hiking directions: Cross the road and head south past the trail sign and metal gate. Ascend a steep hill for the first 100 yards. Continue south along the ridge between two ravines. A stream flows through the drainage on the right. At 1.2 miles, the trail crosses under power poles to a signed junction. The right fork heads west to the Arroyo Burro Trail. Go east on the left fork, towards Gibraltar Road and Matias Potrero Camp, to a second junction at 0.2 miles. The right fork (the main trail) continues to Gibraltar Road. Take the left fork downhill to Matias Potrero Camp. The trail continues beyond the camp and rejoins the main trail. To return, take the same path back.

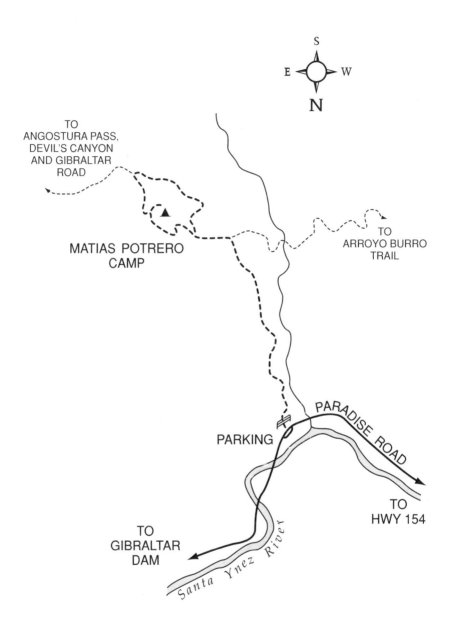

MATIAS POTRERO TRAIL

Hike 40
Lower Oso Trail

Hiking distance: 2 miles round trip
Hiking time: 1 hour
Elevation gain: 200 feet
Maps: Santa Barbara Front Country Recreational Map
U.S.G.S. San Marcos Pass

Summary of hike: The Lower Oso Trail is a short meander at the mouth of Oso Canyon. The trail winds through a beautiful meadow along the banks of Oso Creek, connecting the Lower and Upper Oso Campgrounds.

Driving directions: From Highway 101 in Santa Barbara, take the State Street/Highway 154 exit. Turn right on Highway 154 (San Marcos Pass Road), and drive 10.6 miles to Paradise Road on the right. Turn right and continue 5.8 miles to the Lower Oso Campground on the left. The campground is just beyond the first crossing of the Santa Ynez River. Park in the lot on the right, across from the junction with Romero Camuesa Road.

Hiking directions: From the parking area, hike up the paved Romero Camuesa Road, parallel to Oso Creek, towards Upper Oso Campground. At 0.3 miles, the road crosses a bridge. After crossing, leave the road on a footpath to the left. Cross Oso Creek and follow the path through the forested meadow along the west side of the creek. At 1.2 miles, the trail crosses the creek again and heads into Upper Oso Campground. This is the turnaround spot.

To hike further, continue to the next hike (Hike 41), which begins in Upper Oso Campground.

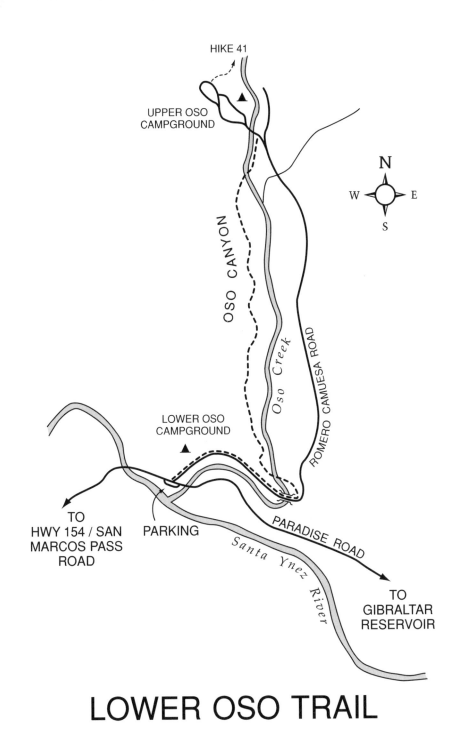

HIKE 41

UPPER OSO
CAMPGROUND

N
W   E
S

OSO CANYON

Oso Creek

ROMERO CAMUESA ROAD

LOWER OSO
CAMPGROUND

TO
HWY 154 / SAN
MARCOS PASS
ROAD

PARKING

PARADISE ROAD

Santa Ynez River

TO
GIBRALTAR
RESERVOIR

LOWER OSO TRAIL

Hike 41
Oso Canyon to Nineteen Oaks Camp

Hiking distance: 4 miles round trip
Hiking time: 2 hours
Elevation gain: 550 feet
Maps: Santa Barbara Front Country Recreational Map
      U.S.G.S. San Marcos Pass

Summary of hike: The hike to Nineteen Oaks Camp follows Oso Canyon through the steep sandstone cliffs of Oso Narrows. The trail parallels Oso Creek up the canyon and past pools to the camp, located at the base of Little Pine Mountain. The camp sits on a shady knoll in an oak tree grove with picnic tables, fire pits, and beautiful views down Oso Canyon.

Driving directions: Follow the driving directions for Hike 40. Turn left into Lower Oso Campground on Romero Camuesa Road, and drive one mile to the Upper Oso Campground. Head to the far end of the campground, past the horse corrals.

Hiking directions: Take the Canyon Trail past the gate, and enter the steep-walled canyon. At one mile, after several creek crossings, the lush trail intersects with the Santa Cruz Trail veering off to the left. The Santa Cruz Trail parallels Oso Creek, crossing the creek a few more times past pools and cascades. Various side paths lead downhill to the pools. At 1.8 miles is a signed junction to Nineteen Oaks Camp. The main trail begins its ascent to the summit of Little Pine Mountain. Take the right fork a quarter mile uphill to Nineteen Oaks Camp, located on a knoll overlooking the canyon.

    On the return route, stay on the Santa Cruz Trail until arriving at the Buckhorn Road junction, a short distance past the junction with the Canyon Trail. Take the unpaved Buckhorn Road to the right, returning to the lower end of the Upper Oso Campground. Return through the campground to the trailhead.

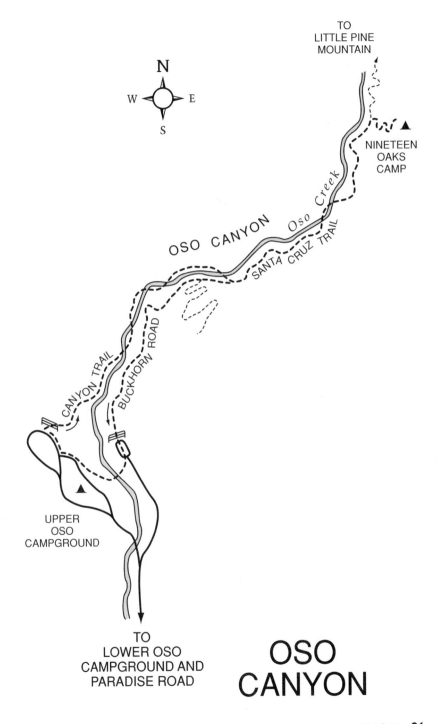

TO
LITTLE PINE
MOUNTAIN

NINETEEN
OAKS
CAMP

OSO CANYON

Oso Creek

SANTA CRUZ TRAIL

CANYON TRAIL

BUCKHORN ROAD

UPPER
OSO
CAMPGROUND

TO
LOWER OSO
CAMPGROUND AND
PARADISE ROAD

OSO CANYON

Hike 42
Aliso Canyon Loop Trail

Hiking distance: 3.5 mile loop
Hiking time: 2 hours
Elevation gain: 800 feet
Maps: Santa Barbara Front Country Recreational Map
U.S.G.S. San Marcos Pass

Summary of hike: The Aliso Canyon Loop Trail begins on a one-mile interpretive trail along Aliso Creek. The trail crosses and recrosses the creek continuously up stream. The trail climbs to a grassy plateau dividing Aliso Canyon and Oso Canyon with views overlooking the Santa Ynez River Valley and the surrounding mountains.

Driving directions: From Highway 101 in Santa Barbara, take the State Street/Highway 154 exit. Turn right on Highway 154 (San Marcos Pass Road), and drive 10.6 miles to Paradise Road on the right. Turn right and continue 4.5 miles to the Los Prietos Ranger Station on the left. Turn left and follow the park road to the Sage Hill Campground. Park in the upper east end of the campground.

Hiking directions: Hike north into the forested canyon. At a quarter mile, after several creek crossings, is a junction with the Aliso Loop Trail, the return route. Continue straight ahead, crossing the creek numerous times and winding up the canyon. Just past sign post #15, the trail heads over a small sage-covered hill before dropping back down to the creek. Cross the creek to a junction with the Aliso Loop Trail at one mile. Ascend the eastern hillside of the canyon to the right, away from the creek. The trail climbs steadily for a half mile to a grassy meadow and a junction with a trail heading left (east) to Upper Oso Campground. Take the right fork, traversing the ridge that divides the canyons. Switchbacks descend back into Aliso Canyon. Rejoin the interpretive trail, and return to the trailhead.

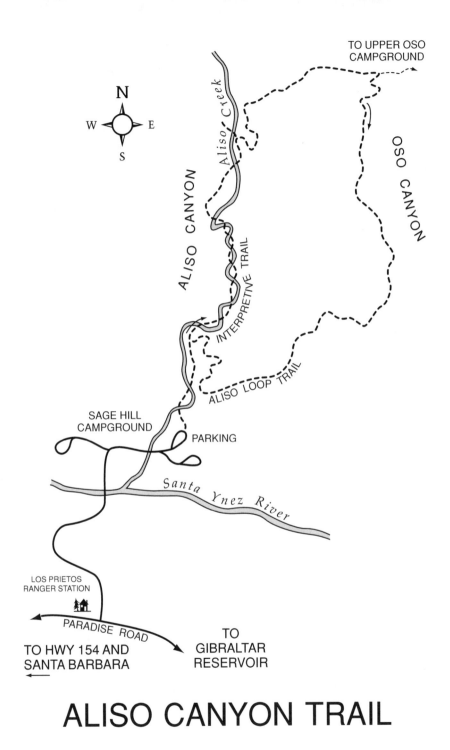

ALISO CANYON TRAIL

Hike 43
Snyder Trail to Knapp's Castle

Hiking distance: 6.6 miles round trip
Hiking time: 3.5 hours
Elevation gain: 2,000 feet
Maps: Santa Barbara Front Country Recreational Map
U.S.G.S. San Marcos Pass

Summary of hike: The Snyder Trail is a longer, steeper trail to Knapp's Castle than the easy stroll from East Camino Cielo Road (Hike 29). This route begins from Paradise Road in the Santa Ynez Valley and heads up to the ridge alongside Lewis Canyon. The hike begins on a service road but narrows to a footpath. A description of Knapp's Castle is on page 66.

Driving directions: From Highway 101 in Santa Barbara, take the State Street/Highway 154 exit. Turn right on Highway 154 (San Marcos Pass Road), and drive 10.6 miles to Paradise Road on the right. Turn right and continue 4.2 miles to the turnout on the right by a "No Vehicle" gate. Park in the turnout. If you reach the Los Prietos Ranger Station, you have gone a little too far.

Hiking directions: From the turnout, hike past the gate on the unpaved road. Fifty yards ahead is the Snyder Trail sign. Stay on the service road past a water tank to a trail split at 0.3 miles. Bear to the right. At 0.7 miles is another water tank on the left and a trail split. Go left on the footpath. The trail gains elevation via switchbacks through a forested area, then heads across grassy slopes and knolls to scenic overlooks. Along the way, the views get better and the knolls offer stopping spots. At 1.8 miles, the Snyder Trail ends at a junction with Knapp Road. Take the road to the right as it curves around the contours of the hillside. At 3.1 miles the trail joins an unpaved road that leads to East Camino Cielo Road. Take the unpaved road to the left, and pass the "Private Property" gate to Knapp's Castle.

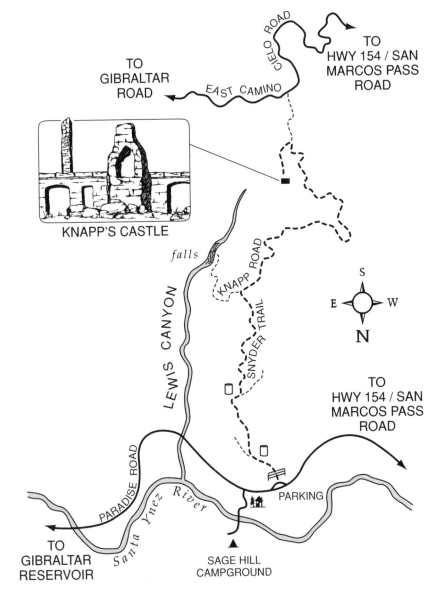

KNAPP'S CASTLE

SNYDER TRAIL
TO KNAPP'S CASTLE

Hike 44
Tequepis Canyon

Hiking distance: 2 miles round trip
Hiking time: 1 hour
Elevation gain: 500 feet
Maps: The Cachuma Lake Recreation Area map
       U.S.G.S. Lake Cachuma

Summary of hike: The Tequepis Canyon hike follows the first section of the Tequepis Trail, which leads out of the canyon to West Camino Cielo Road, gaining 2,300 feet in four miles. The trail is well defined yet not heavily used. This hike parallels Tequepis Creek up canyon for one mile through a shady oak and sycamore forest. The trail crosses the creek three times.

Driving directions: From Highway 101 in Santa Barbara, take the State Street/Highway 154 exit. Turn right on Highway 154 (San Marcos Pass Road), and drive 16.9 miles to the signed turnoff for Ranch Alegre and Camp Whittier on the left. Turn left and continue 1.3 miles to the road's end at the designated parking area on the right.

Hiking directions: From the parking area, follow the paved road past the Tequepis Trail sign and ranch gate. Continue past the swimming pool to the Tequepis Trailhead at a signed junction. The paved road curves to the right. Take the trail bearing left, past the camp cabins and across Tequepis Creek. The trail crosses the creek a second time at 0.4 miles. Boulder hop across and continue south, remaining close to Tequepis Creek. At 0.6 miles, the trail crosses to the east side of the creek for the final crossing. At one mile, the trail narrows and sharply turns left, leaving the creek and beginning the ascent out of the canyon. This is the turnaround spot.

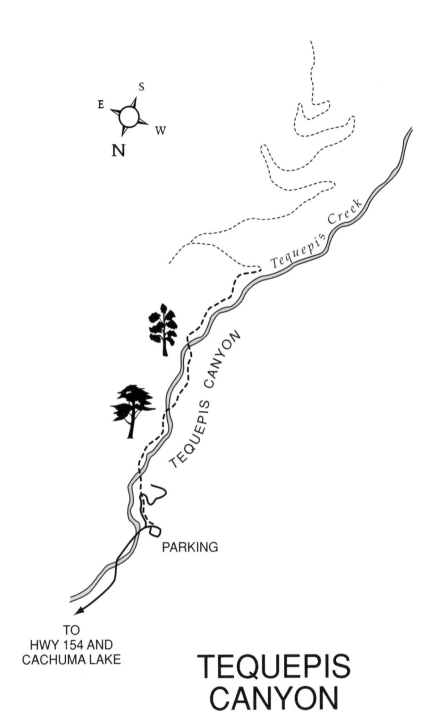

S
E   W
N

Tequepis Creek

TEQUEPIS CANYON

PARKING

TO
HWY 154 AND
CACHUMA LAKE

TEQUEPIS
CANYON

Hike 45
Mohawk Mesa Trail
Cachuma Lake

Hiking distance: 0.6 mile loop
Hiking time: 15 minutes
Elevation gain: Level
Maps: The Cachuma Lake Recreation Area map
   U.S.G.S. Lake Cachuma

Summary of hike: The Mohawk Mesa Trail is a short, charming loop around a lakeside peninsula jutting into Cachuma Lake. The trail follows the perimeter of the land, circling around Mohawk Mesa. At the northern tip is Mohawk Point and a fishing pier.

Driving directions: From Highway 101 in Santa Barbara, take the State Street/Highway 154 exit. Turn right on Highway 154 (San Marcos Pass Road), and drive 17.5 miles to the Cachuma Lake County Park entrance on the right. Turn right and continue past the entrance kiosk straight ahead 0.1 mile. Turn right, following the signs to the Overflow Area. Continue 0.5 miles to the signed Mohawk Mesa Trail on the left. Park in the pullout by the trailhead.

Hiking directions: From the parking pullout, hike beside the northeast edge of Mohawk Mesa along Martini Cove. The forested path leads to Mohawk Point, overlooking Cachuma Lake on three sides. Near the northernmost point is a fishing pier. Along the way, several side paths lead down to the water's edge. The trail returns beside Drake Cove, a small, quiet inlet. Back at the park road, return to the trailhead on the left.

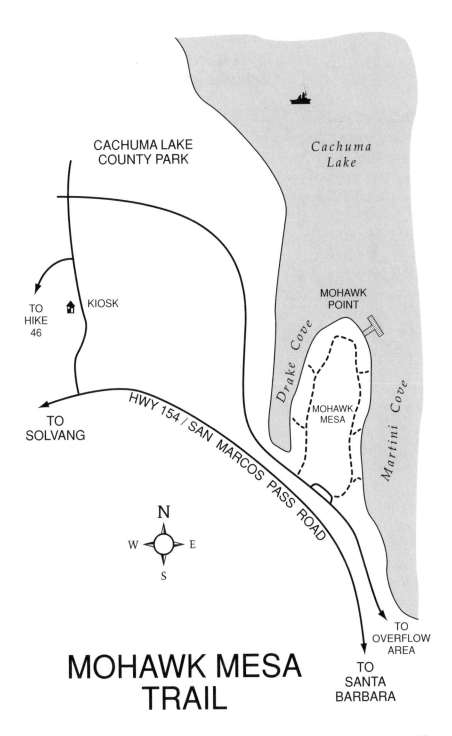

CACHUMA LAKE
COUNTY PARK

Cachuma Lake

TO
HIKE
46

KIOSK

MOHAWK
POINT

Drake Cove

HWY 154 / SAN MARCOS PASS ROAD

TO
SOLVANG

MOHAWK
MESA

Martini Cove

N

W   E

S

TO
OVERFLOW
AREA

TO
SANTA
BARBARA

MOHAWK MESA TRAIL

Hike 46
Sweetwater Trail to Vista Point
Cachuma Lake

Hiking distance: 5 miles round trip
Hiking time: 2.5 hours
Elevation gain: 160 feet
Maps: The Cachuma Lake Recreation Area map
U.S.G.S. Lake Cachuma

Summary of hike: The 2.5 mile Sweetwater Trail begins at Harvey's Cove in Cachuma Lake, a beautiful cove with a handicap-accessible fishing dock and picnic area under a grove of oak trees. The trail ends at Vista Point and Bradbury Dam, a scenic overlook near the west end of the lake. Along the way, the trail hugs the shoreline around inlets and coves, passes lake overlooks, and meanders through an oak forest.

Driving directions: Follow the driving directions for Hike 45 to Cachuma Lake County Park. Turn into the park, and continue past the entrance kiosk. Take the road to the left for 0.3 miles to the trailhead parking lot at the road's end, following the signs to Harvey's Cove.

Hiking directions: From the parking lot, take the paved path around the south shoreline of Harvey's Cove. As you near the pier, take the hiking trail veering off to the left. The trail stays close to the water's edge, curving around each inlet. Once past Harvey's Cove, the trail curves inland and gains elevation, soon arriving at the Sweetwater Picnic Area. From the picnic area, follow the trail past the Vista Point sign, curving completely around Sweetwater Cove. At the south end of the cove, the trail joins an unpaved road for a short distance before picking up the trail again on the right and crossing a bridge. At 2.5 miles, the trail ends at the Vista Point parking lot and an overlook of the Bradbury Dam. Return along the same trail.

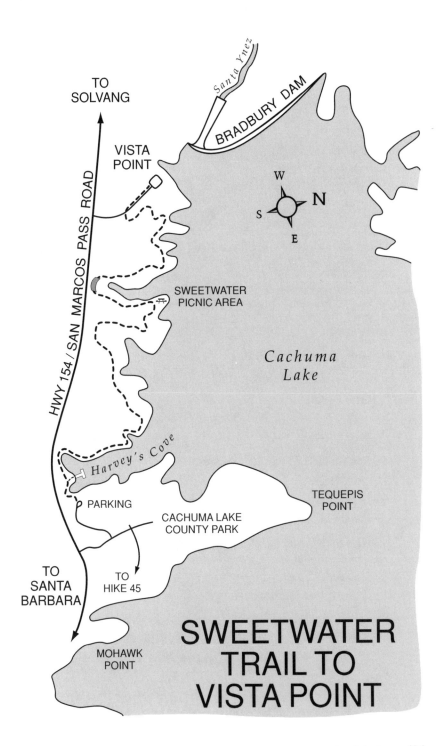

TO
SOLVANG

VISTA
POINT

Santa Ynez

BRADBURY DAM

HWY 154 / SAN MARCOS PASS ROAD

W N
S E

SWEETWATER
PICNIC AREA

*Cachuma
Lake*

Harvey's Cove

PARKING

CACHUMA LAKE
COUNTY PARK

TEQUEPIS
POINT

TO
SANTA
BARBARA

TO
HIKE 45

MOHAWK
POINT

SWEETWATER
TRAIL TO
VISTA POINT

Other Day Hike Guidebooks

___ Day Hikes on Oahu $9.95

___ Day Hikes on Maui 8.95

___ Day Hikes on Kauai 8.95

___ Day Hikes in Yosemite National Park
25 Favorite Hikes 8.95

___ Day Hikes Around Lake Tahoe 8.95

___ Day Hikes in Los Angeles
Malibu to Hollywood 8.95

___ Day Hikes Around Santa Barbara, California 11.95

___ Day Hikes in Ventura County, California 11.95

___ Day Hikes Around Denver, Colorado 9.95

___ Day Hikes in Aspen, Colorado 7.95

___ Day Hikes in Boulder, Colorado 8.95

___ Day Hikes in Steamboat Springs, Colorado 8.95

___ Day Hikes in Summit County, Colorado 8.95

___ Day Hikes in Yellowstone National Park
25 Favorite Hikes 8.95

___ Day Hikes in Grand Teton National Park and Jackson Hole 8.95

___ Day Hikes in the Beartooth Mountains
Red Lodge, Montana to Yellowstone National Park 8.95

___ Day Hikes Around Bozeman, Montana 9.95

___ Day Hikes Around Missoula, Montana 9.95

___ Day Hikes in Sedona, Arizona
25 Favorite Hikes 9.95

___ Day Trips on St. Martin 9.95

These books may be purchased at your local bookstore or
outdoor shop. Or, order them direct from the distributor:

The Globe Pequot Press
P.O. Box 833 · Old Saybrook, CT 06475
www.globe-pequot.com

1-800-243-0495

Notes